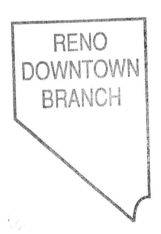

MAKE YOUR OWN
Performing
Puppets

Teddy Cameron Long

A Sterling/Tamos Book
Sterling Publishing Co., Inc. New York

A Sterling/Tamos Book
© 1995 Teddy Cameron Long

Sterling Publishing Company, Inc.
387 Park Avenue South, New York, NY 10016

TAMOS Books Inc.
300 Wales Avenue, Winnipeg, MB, Canada R2M 2S9

10 9 8 7 6 5 4 3 2 1

Distributed in Canada by Sterling Publishing Co., Inc.
c/o Canadian Manda Group, P.O. Box 920, Station U
Toronto, Ontario, Canada M8Z 5P9
Distributed in Great Britain and Europe by Cassell PLC
Villiers House, 41/47 Strand, London WC2N 5JE, England
Distributed in Australia by Capricorn Link (Australia) Pty Ltd.
P.O. Box 6651, Baulkham Hills, Business Centre, NSW 2153,
Australia

Projects and Illustrations Teddy Cameron Long
Photography Jerry Grajewski, Jerry Kopelow,
      KKS Commercial Photography
Design A.O. Osen

Library of Congress Cataloging-in-Publication Data
Long, Teddy Cameron.
      Make your own performing puppets/Teddy Cameron Long
            p.   cm.
      "A Sterling/Tamos book."
      Includes index.
      ISBN 1-895569-32-X
      1. Puppet making--Juvenile literature. [1. Puppet making.]
I. Title
TT174.7.L66   1995
745.592'24--dc20   94-35536
                                                    CIP
                                                    AC

Canadian Cataloguing-in-Publication Data
Long, Teddy Cameron
      Make your own performing puppets
      "A Sterling/Tamos book."
      Includes index.
      ISBN 1-895569-32-X
1. Puppet making. I. Title.
TT174.7.L65 1995   745.592'24   C94-920205-3

Printed in China

Contents

Introduction

Homemade and handcrafted puppets can turn a theatrical production into something special. Add your creative touch to paper, glue, paint, cloth, dough, wooden spoons, and other household items and you'll produce spectacular results.

Choose from several different techniques to make your production the best it can be. Each project has complete instructions with detailed diagrams to guide you every step of the way. Color photographs of the projects provide suggestions for finishing and show you some of the steps along the way. Choose projects that suit your performance— from amazing marionettes to players' costumes to body painting to shadow puppets to felt board characters for storytelling. You'll find a great selection and any of these unusual crafts will help put you in the theatrical mood.

Materials

All materials used in these projects are easily found around the home, or obtained from a craft shop or hardware store. They are not expensive and leftover supplies can always be used later for other craft or school projects. The projects here are meant as suggestions. Your imagination and creativity make anything possible. Have fun!

Not all materials or tools are needed for each project. Protect working surfaces with a plastic sheet or newspaper.

Paper brown paper lunch bags or grocery bags, newspaper, large sheets of paper from a roll, bond paper

Glue white carpenter's or craft glue, fabric glue, hot or warm melt glue gun, wallpaper paste (powder form must be mixed according to package directions)

Cardboard strong cardboard boxes (from grocery or hardware stores), thin cardboard (from cereal boxes), flexible cardboard (smooth one side and rippled one side), cardboard tubes (toilet tissue tubes, paper towel tubes, wrapping paper tubes)

Paint powdered poster paint, acrylic paint, face paint, shellac (to protect powder paint surface), methyl hydrate (to clean shellac from brushes)

Tools scissors, pencils, markers, masking tape, string, paper clips, push pins, thin wooden rods (barbeque skewers with pointed ends cut off for younger children), brushes, containers for mixing paints (old muffin tin, plastic or tin cans)

Miscellaneous flour dough, wooden spoons, colored felt pieces, fabric, socks, needles, thread, yarn, balloons, glitter, rhinestones, feathers, chenille stems, bandaids (to attach props to hands), foam blocks (used in cushions)

RUSH SEATS $.50

Rainforest

SAT. MAY 7   8:00 PM

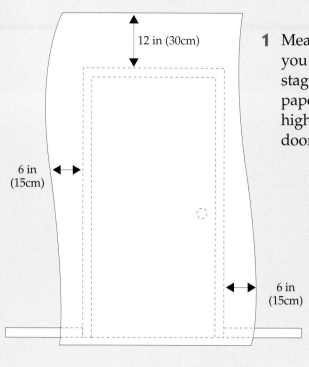

1 Measure the doorway you will use for the stage. Make a sheet of paper wider and higher than the doorway, as shown.

DOORWAY SCREEN MATERIALS
large sheets of paper
glue
ruler
pencil
scissors
newspaper
masking tape
push pins
paint
brushes
shellac

2 Choose a comfortable height for the puppet players to work the puppets. If that is 30 in (76cm), then cut that amount from the bottom of the sheet.

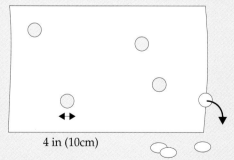

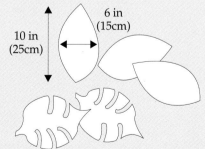

3 In the bottom sheet, cut out four holes, as shown.

4 From extra paper draw and cut out large leaves, as shown.

5 Glue the leaves to the paper screen loosely covering three of the holes in the screen. Hands will push through the holes and out the paper leaves, as shown. Leave one hole uncovered.

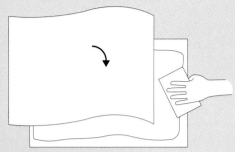

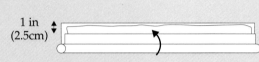

6 Make a thick branch for under the uncovered hole. Spread glue on a single sheet of newspaper and place another sheet 1 in (2.5cm) from the top of the first sheet.

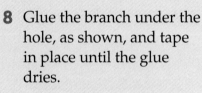

1 in (2.5cm)

7 Starting from the bottom, roll into a tube and twist into a rope, as shown.

8 Glue the branch under the hole, as shown, and tape in place until the glue dries.

9 Make twigs using one single sheet of paper and glue, then follow Step 7. Glue and tape to the lower sheet, as desired. *See* photo at right.

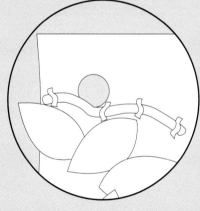

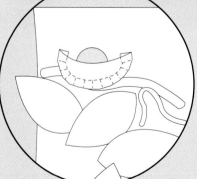

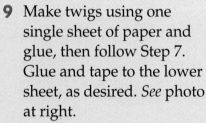

8 in (20cm)

6 in (15cm)

1/2 in (1cm)

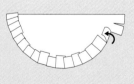

10 To make a bird's nest, cut a half circle of paper and make cuts all around the rounded side, as shown.

11 Fold the cut tabs over.

12 Glue the cut tabs to the paper around the uncovered hole, as shown. Tape in place. A bird puppet can be worked through this hole and appear to be in the nest.

14 Paint the two sheets of paper to resemble a rainforest. The bottom sheet is the foreground of a rainforest and the top sheet is the background sky. Protect wall and floor surfaces with plastic or newspaper. Hang the paper on top of the plastic or newspaper with push-pins. Draw and paint the scenery. Shellac. *See* photograph, p6.

4 in (10cm)

2 in (5cm)

TO PERFORM

The puppet players stand behind the doorway and work the hand puppets up between the two paper screens and also through the holes cut in the bottom screens. Act out a story about the rainforest with forest creature puppets.

13 Cut out more leaves and glue them to the bottom sheet and to the lowest area of the top sheet, as shown.

15 Hang the painted screens on the doorway with masking tape. Place the bottom piece in front of the doorway facing the audience. Place the top piece behind the door, overlapping the bottom piece about 6 in (15cm).

PAINTED HAND PUPPETS MATERIALS
costume face paint
yarn
feathers
twigs

PAINTED HAND PUPPETS

1 **PERSON**—Hold the index finger and middle finger out straight and curl up the remaining fingers and thumb behind them. Cut off the sticky tab of a band-aid and roll it into a loop, sticky side out. Use this sticky loop to attach 3 in (7.6cm) strands of wool to the back of the hand near the wrist. This is hair. Paint a face below the hair. Paint the fingers to resemble pants. Paint the space on the hand between the face and the pants to resemble a shirt. *See* photo.

2 **SPIDER**—Cut two chenille stems each 6 in (15cm) long. Curl up one end of each stem. Bend 1/2 in (1.3cm) of the other end of each stem and tape to the back of the hand, near the wrist. These are antennae. Paint eyes and a mouth on the back of the hand near the knuckles. Paint stripes around the fingers, and fill in the rest of the hand with a bright color. *See* photo.

3 **ANIMALS**— To make an animal head and neck make a fist with the thumb on the outside of the fingers. Paint pink around the inside of the thumb and fingers for the mouth.

4 DEER—Paint eyes on the backs of the index and pinkie fingers. Paint a black nose on the middle two fingers. Paint the rest of the hand with brown strokes and white spots. Place two twigs between the fingers for antlers. *See* photo.

5 SNAKE—Paint an eye on each side of the hand. Paint diamond shapes down the back of the hand and arm. Fill in the rest with bright colors. *See* photo.

6 LEOPARD—Paint green eyes on the back of the hand next to the knuckles. Paint the rest of the hand and arm yellow. Paint black ears on the back of the hand and black semi-circles over the rest of the puppet. Paint brown spots in the center of the black semi-circles. Cut black chenille stems 6 in (15cm) long. Wrap the ends of three stems around the middle finger and three other stems around the ring finger for whiskers. *See* photo.

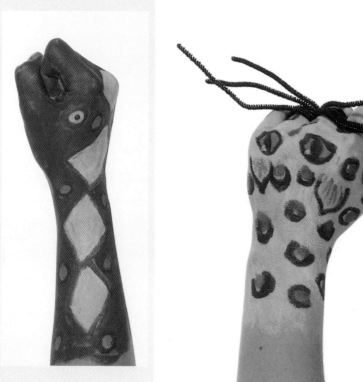

7 PARROT—Paint all the fingers and thumb yellow to the knuckles. Draw a black line where the yellow paint ends. This is the beak. Draw an eye on the side of the hand, next to the black line. Attach feathers to the back of the hand using band-aids. Paint more feather shapes on the hand and arm, covering the band-aids as well. *See* photo.

11

RUSH SEATS $.50

Slay the Dragon

SAT. OCT 7 8:00 PM

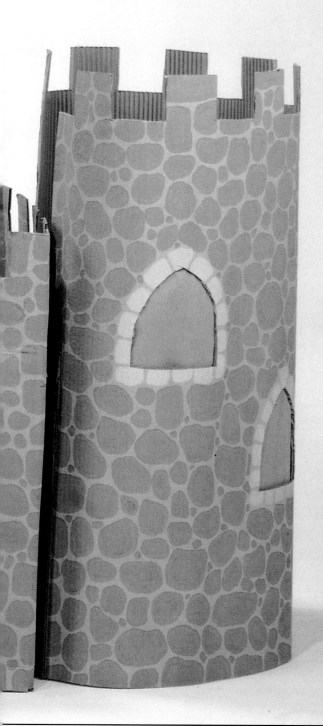

THEATER BOX MATERIALS

large cardboard box
ruler
pencil
scissors
glue
brown paper
flexible rippled
   cardboard
velcro
masking tape
paint
brushes
shellac

1 Use one large cardboard box or two smaller boxes joined together, as shown below. Cut off the flap of one long side on each box. Cut down the center of that same side and along the bottom, as shown.

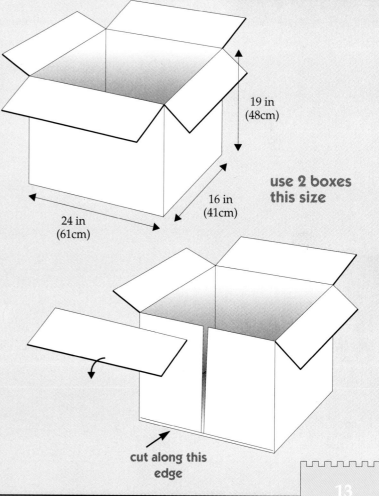

19 in
(48cm)

16 in
(41cm)

24 in
(61cm)

use 2 boxes this size

cut along this edge

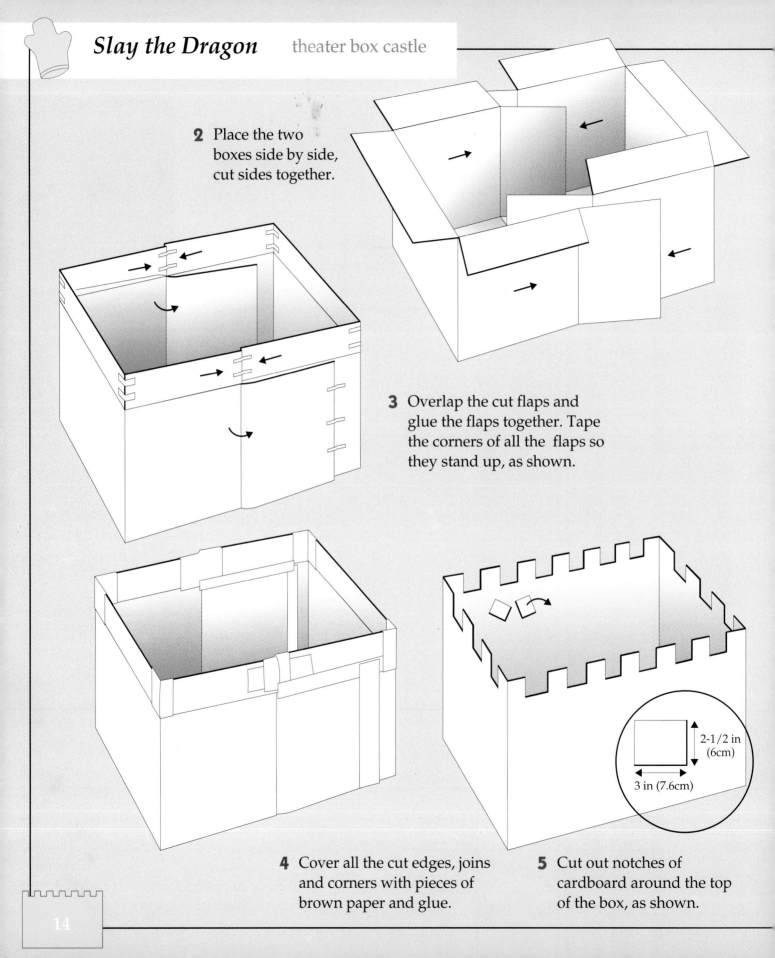

2 Place the two boxes side by side, cut sides together.

3 Overlap the cut flaps and glue the flaps together. Tape the corners of all the flaps so they stand up, as shown.

4 Cover all the cut edges, joins and corners with pieces of brown paper and glue.

5 Cut out notches of cardboard around the top of the box, as shown.

2-1/2 in (6cm)

3 in (7.6cm)

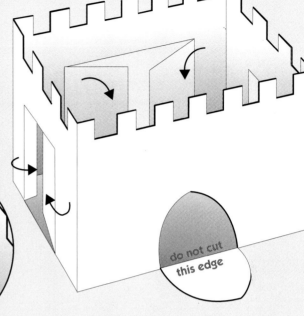

6 Cut a drawbridge door out of the front of the castle, as shown. Do not cut along the bottom side. Cut doorways out of the back and both side walls, as shown. The doorway at the back should be large enough for a puppet player to crawl through.

7 Fold the side doors right back against the wall and glue in place.

side doors detail

drawbridge detail

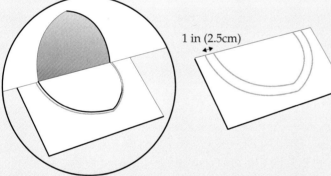

1 in (2.5cm)

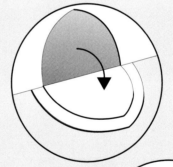

8 Lay a piece of cardboard under the open drawbridge and trace around it, as shown.

9 Remove the cardboard, and draw a larger drawbridge around the first one, as shown. Cut out.

10 Glue the larger cardboard drawbridge to the one on the castle, as shown.

11 Close the drawbridge. Punch a hole through the side of the drawbridge and the castle wall on each side, as shown. Cut two pieces of string 18 in (45cm) long. Thread one piece through each hole. Tie a knot outside the door, and the other knot inside the castle. The drawbridge can now go up and down.

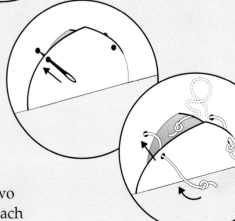

11 Make two towers, one for each side. Use flexible rippled cardboard. Cut two sheets, as shown, and cut notches along one long side of each sheet, as shown.

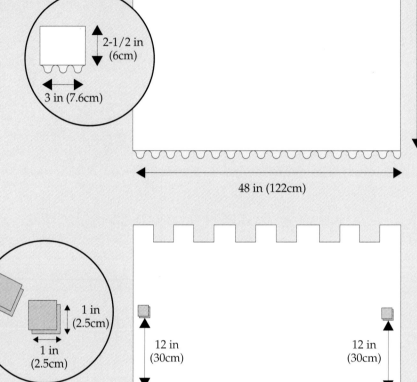

2-1/2 in (6cm)

3 in (7.6cm)

33 in (84cm)

48 in (122cm)

12 Attach the towers to the castle with velcro. Cut four square pieces of velcro, as shown, for each tower.

1 in (2.5cm)

1 in (2.5cm)

12 in (30cm)

12 in (30cm)

13 Glue the velcro to the smooth side of each end of the tower, as shown.

14 Matching velcro squares must be attached to either side of the openings on the castle sides. Spread glue on the tower velcro squares, and press the towers into position.

15 Separate the velcro pieces and press the glued half of each piece onto the glued spot on the castle wall. Tape in place until the glue dries.

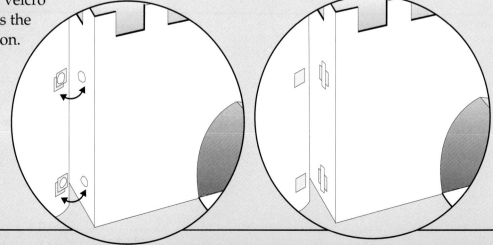

TO PERFORM

One puppet player wears the dragon helmet and is this character in the play. The other players are inside the castle and towers and work the cloth hand puppets to act out a story involving the dragon. The doorways are large enough for puppet players to go in and out as required.

CLOTH PUPPETS MATERIALS
sheet of paper
pencil
scissors
plain white cloth
  (T-shirt material)
scissors
straight pins
white thread
needle
acrylic paint or
  fabric paint
yarn
rhinestones
glitter

16 Cut out windows in the front side of the towers and castle wall. *See* photo above. Inside the box, glue pieces of cloth above the windows to cover the holes, *see* photo, p12.

17 Paint the castle and towers. Shellac.

CLOTH PUPPETS

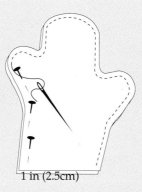

1 in (2.5cm)

1 To make a pattern that will fit a hand, trace around the hand on a piece of paper. Hold the hand flat, as shown, with the thumb and little finger extended.

2 Draw a puppet shape around the hand tracing, leaving a border, as shown. Cut out the pattern.

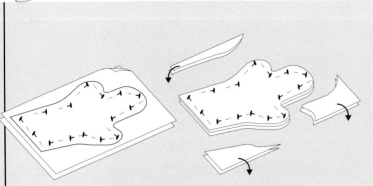

unsewn edge

3 Place two pieces of white cloth, right sides together, as shown. Place the paper pattern on top and pin all three layers together.

4 Cut around the pattern, making two cloth shapes. Remove the paper pattern.

5 Pin the two cloth shapes, right sides together and sew around the edges of the cloth leaving the bottom edge unsewn.

6 If the fabric requires a hem, turn the bottom edges up 1/4 in (.6cm) and pin. Sew the hem, leaving the bottom open, as shown. Turn the puppet right sides out.

7 Paint the cloth with acrylic paint or fabric paint.

8 When dry, glue on yarn for hair, rhinestones, or glitter, as desired.

NOTE

Make additional puppets for the performance using the same basic technique as for the cloth puppet described. Apply different painted faces and costumes to create new characters for the play. *See* examples in the photograph.

DRAGON HELMET

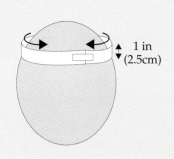

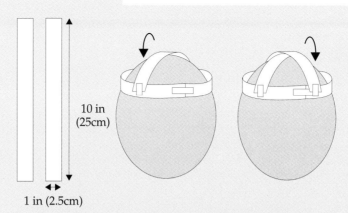

1 in (2.5cm)

10 in (25cm)

1 in (2.5cm)

DRAGON HELMET MATERIALS

thin cardboard
scissors
ruler
pencil
masking tape
glue
egg carton
newspaper strips
wallpaper paste
paint
brushes
shellac

1 From thin cardboard (cereal boxes) cut a strip, as shown, to fit around the puppet player's head. Tape in place.

2 Cut two more strips of cardboard, as shown.

3 Tape one strip end to the front of the head band and bend it up and across to the back of the head, as shown. Trim to fit and tape in place.

4 Tape the second strip end to the side of the head band and bend up and across the head in the same way, making a cross, as shown. Trim to fit and tape in place. Remove the cap from the head.

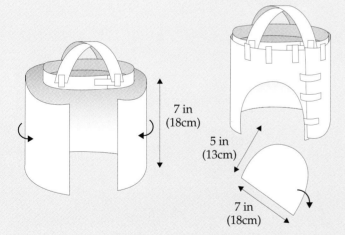

7 in (18cm)

5 in (13cm)

7 in (18cm)

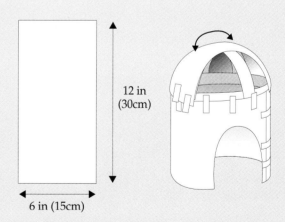

12 in (30cm)

6 in (15cm)

5 Cut another piece of cardboard long enough to wrap around the cap, as shown.

6 Wrap the piece around the cap, taping the ends together and the top edge of the sheet to the cardboard band, as shown. Cut a half-circle out of the front of the cardboard, as shown.

7 Cut another piece of cardboard, as shown.

8 Fold this piece of cardboard over the top of the cap and tape the ends to either side, as shown, to make a helmet.

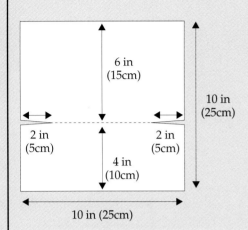

9 Cut another piece of cardboard, as shown. Make a fold and a cut along each end of the fold, as shown.

10 Place this piece of cardboard across the front of the helmet, as shown.

11 Wrap the ends of the top section around the sides of the helmet, as shown. Tape in place.

12 Roll the bottom section into a cone, and tape to form a snout. Tape the corners to the helmet, as shown.

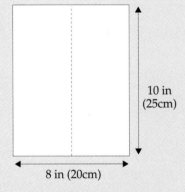

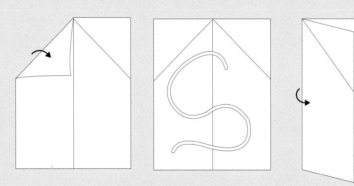

13 Cut another piece of cardboard and fold in half, as shown.

14 Fold each top corner over to the middle, as shown.

15 Lay the piece flat and spread glue over the bottom two sections.

16 Fold in half again, glued sides together. Let the glue dry.

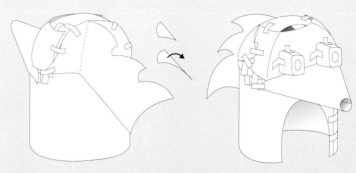

17 Fold the corners against the back of the helmet, as shown, covering the back opening, and tape in place.

18 Trim the protruding section of this piece into spines, as shown.

19 Cut off two egg cups from an egg carton, and tape these to the front of the helmet for dragon eyes.

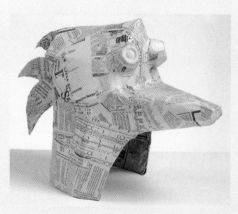

20 Cover the entire helmet with strips of newspaper dipped in wallpaper paste. Set aside to dry. Paint and shellac.

**CIRCUS
BACKDROP
MATERIALS**
**large sheets of paper
ruler
pencil
scissors
masking tape
push pins
glue
paint
brushes
shellac**

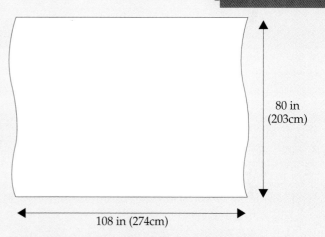

80 in
(203cm)

108 in (274cm)

1 Use very large sheets of paper or glue
together smaller pieces to make two
large sheets. Cut one sheet to the
measurements shown.

A sheet this size will be quite heavy,
especially when wet with paint, so it
needs reinforcement.

2 Cut four pieces
of masking
tape, as
shown,
and stick
one on top of
another.

1 in
(2.5cm)

1 in
(2.5cm)

23

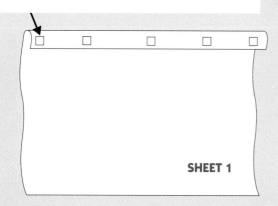

SHEET 1

3 Stick this pad of tape to the back of the sheet in a top corner. Make four more masking tape pads and stick them along the top edge, as shown.

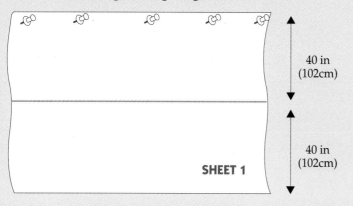

40 in (102cm)

40 in (102cm)

SHEET 1

5 Measure and draw a line across the middle of the sheet.

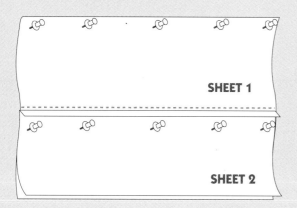

SHEET 1

SHEET 2

8 Place the folded edge of sheet 2 along the drawn line on sheet 1 and pin sheet 2 to sheet 1 below the folded edge, as shown.

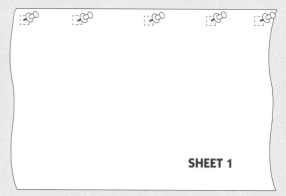

SHEET 1

4 Hang the paper on a wall by sticking push pins through the paper and tape, into the wall. *See* note, p25.

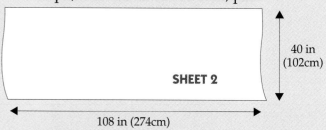

40 in (102cm)

SHEET 2

108 in (274cm)

6 Cut another sheet of paper, as shown.

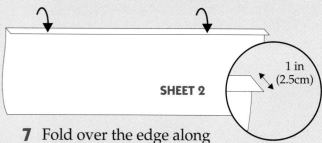

1 in (2.5cm)

SHEET 2

7 Fold over the edge along one long side, as shown.

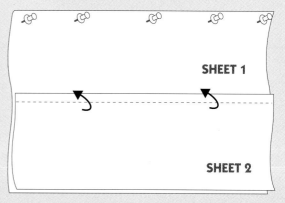

SHEET 1

SHEET 2

9 Spread glue along the folded edge and fold this glued edge back onto sheet 1 and smooth in place, as shown.

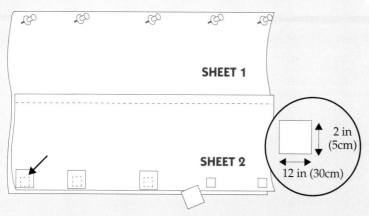

SHEET 1

SHEET 2

2 in (5cm)

12 in (30cm)

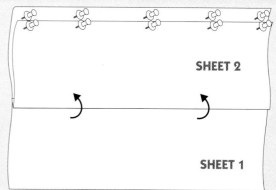

SHEET 2

SHEET 1

10 Remove the pins from sheet 2. Make five more masking tape pads as in Step 2, and stick these along the bottom edge of sheet 2. Cut five pieces of paper, as shown, and glue one paper square over each masking tape pad. (This will allow you to paint over them later).

11 Fold sheet 2 up and pin the bottom edge of sheet 2 directly beneath the pins of sheet 1, as shown. Push the pins through the masking tape pads, into the wall.

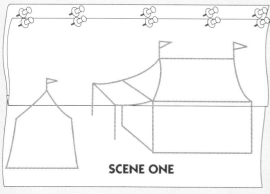

SCENE ONE

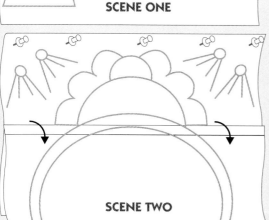

SCENE TWO

12 Draw and paint scene one over the back of sheet 2 and the bottom half of sheet 1, as shown. Shellac. Allow to dry.

13 Remove the pins holding up sheet 2 and let it drop down. Draw and paint scene two over the top half of sheet 1 and the front of sheet 2, as shown. Shellac. Allow to dry.

The mottled grass and sand in the photographs were created with a sea sponge dipped in paint and dabbed against the paper. *See* materials p4–5.

TO PERFORM

The puppet player dresses as a character in the play, the ringmaster, and works the puppets in full view.

To perform in front of the backdrop, begin with sheet 2 pinned up and scene one showing. To change the backdrop, simply remove the pins in sheet 2 and let it drop down.

NOTE If it is not possible to hang the sheets on the wall with push pins, adapt the technique to your situation. Two suggestions: suspend a board from the ceiling to attach the backdrops, or lean sheets of particle board against the wall and attach the backdrops. Tape will not be strong enough to hold the weight of the painted backdrops.

RINGMASTER TUNIC

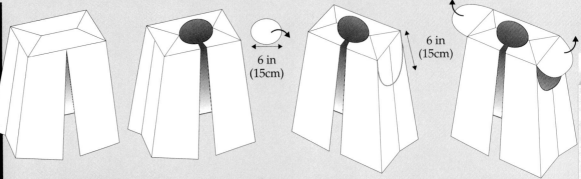

6 in (15cm)

6 in (15cm)

RINGMASTER TUNIC MATERIALS

brown paper bag
ruler
pencil
scissors
paint
brushes
shellac

1 Open a brown paper grocery bag and make a cut up the center of one wide side, as shown. Cut a circle in the center of the bottom, as shown.

2 On each side of the bag, draw a scooped shape, as shown. Cut around each shape, creating flaps attached at the folded edge, as shown.

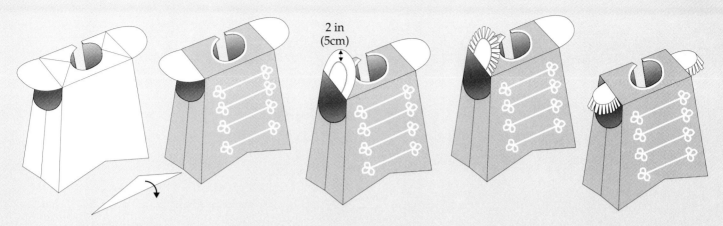

3 On the uncut wide side, cut out a V-shape, as shown.

4 Paint the bag to resemble a ringmaster's uniform. Paint both sides of the shoulder tabs yellow. Shellac. When the shellac is dry, fold the shoulder tabs back. Draw another arched shape, as shown.

5 Cut to form a fringe, as shown, and fold the fringe over.

6 Tape the opening at the back closed when wearing the tunic.

RINGMASTER TOP HAT

1 Prepare one double thickness sheet of paper to the measurements shown. Spread glue over one sheet and place another sheet over the first and smooth in place.

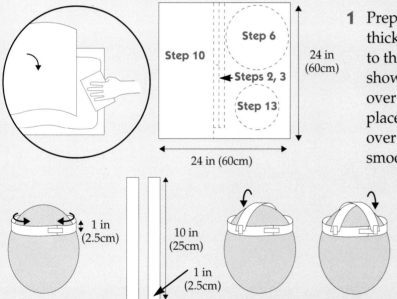

Step 6

Step 10

Steps 2, 3

Step 13

24 in (60cm)

24 in (60cm)

1 in (2.5cm)

10 in (25cm)

1 in (2.5cm)

TOP HAT MATERIALS
paper
glue
ruler
pencil
scissors
masking tape
paint
brushes
shellac

2 From this sheet, cut a strip of paper long enough to wrap around a head, as shown. Fit around the head and tape.

3 Cut two more strips of paper, as shown.

4 Tape one strip end to the front of the band and bend it up and across to the back of the band, as shown. Trim to fit and tape in place.

5 Tape the second strip end to the side of the band and bend it up and across the head, as shown. Trim to fit and tape in place. Remove the cap from the head.

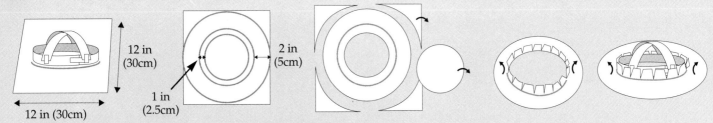

6 Using a square section of the prepared sheet, place the cap on the sheet and trace around it, as shown.

7 Draw another circle outside the first circle, and a third circle inside the first circle, as shown.

8 Cut around the largest circle and cut out the inside circle, as shown.

9 Make cuts around the inside circle 1 in (2.5cm) apart, as shown, and bend the tabs upward. This is the hat brim. Slide the piece over the cap right down to the bottom edge, as shown. Glue the tabs to the outside of the cap.

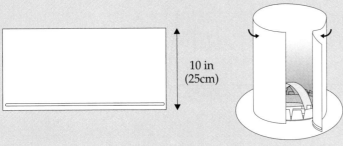

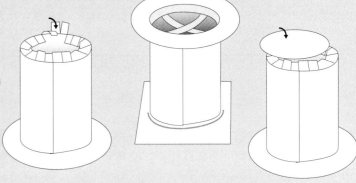

10 Cut a rectangle from the prepared sheet of paper long enough to wrap around the cap. Spread glue along one long side.

11 Wrap the sheet around the cap and glue the edge against the cap, as shown. Glue the ends together. Tape in place until the glue dries.

12 Make 1 in (2.5cm) cuts around the top of the cylinder, and bend the tabs inward.

13 Place the hat upside down on the prepared sheet of paper. Trace around the crown and cut out.

14 Spread glue on the tabs of the hat and place the circle on top. Tape in place until the glue dries. Paint the hat black and shellac. Decorate with glitter, if desired.

METAL LOOP MATERIALS
paper clips
pliers (optional)

METAL LOOPS for STRINGING MARIONETTES

Unfold a paper clip to make a metal loop for stringing the marionette. Fold the smaller, inside loop of the paper clip straight up at a right angle, as shown. Use a pair of pliers, if desired.

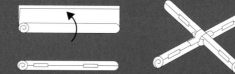

TWO-LEGGED PUPPET CONTROL ROD

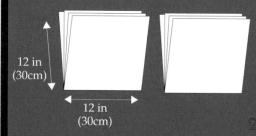

12 in (30cm)

12 in (30cm)

1 To make a control rod for two-legged puppets, use a section of newspaper folded together. Cut the paper into two pieces, as shown.

2 Roll each square into a tight tube and tape.

3 Place one tube over the other to form a cross and tape in place.

4 Cover the tubes with newspaper strips dipped in wallpaper paste. Cover with three or four layers of strips. Set aside to dry. Paint black and shellac.

FOUR-LEGGED PUPPET CONTROL ROD

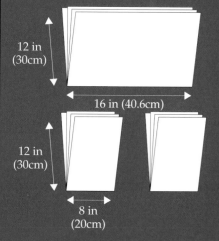

12 in (30cm)

16 in (40.6cm)

12 in (30cm)

8 in (20cm)

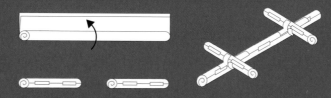

2 Roll each rectangle into a tight tube and tape.

3 Place a short tube across the long tube 3 in (8cm) from each end, as shown. Tape in place.

4 Cover the tubes with newspaper strips dipped in wallpaper paste. Cover with three or four layers of strips. Set aside to dry. Paint black and shellac.

1 To make a control rod for four-legged puppets, use a section of newspaper folded together. Cut the section into three pieces, as shown.

MARIONETTE CONTROL ROD MATERIALS
newspaper
ruler
pencil
scissors
masking tape
newspaper strips
wallpaper paste
paint
brushes
shellac

TRAPEZE ARTIST MATERIALS

newspaper
ruler
pencil
masking tape
cardboard tube
scissors
4 metal loops, p28
newspaper strips
wallpaper paste
cushion foam
marker
utility knife
glue gun or
    5-minute epoxy
paint
brushes
shellac

TRAPEZE ARTIST

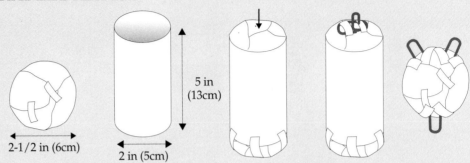

2-1/2 in (6cm)

2 in (5cm)

5 in (13cm)

1 To make the papier-mâché head, crumple a full sheet of newspaper into a ball, as shown. Tape in place.

2 For the body, cut a cardboard tube, as shown.

3 Stuff the tube with newspaper. Allow some newspaper to bulge out the ends of the tube, to make a rounded end. Tape the paper in place.

4 Tape one metal loop to one end of the body tube and tape three other loops to the head, as shown.

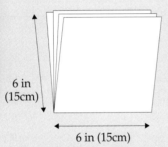

6 in (15cm)

6 in (15cm)

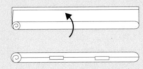

5 To make the trapeze, cut folded newspaper into a square, as shown.

6 Roll into a tight tube and tape in place.

7 Cover the tube, body, and head with strips of newspaper dipped in wallpaper paste. Do not cover the metal loops that stick up from the body, but make sure the loops are well attached to the body, as shown. Set aside to dry.

1 in (2.5cm)

5 in (13cm)

1 in (2.5cm)

8 Using a utility knife, cut four blocks of cushion foam to the measurements shown. The arms and legs of the trapeze artist are cut from these pieces.

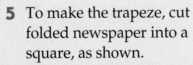

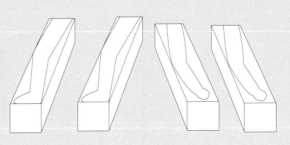

leg

arm

9 Using a marker, draw the legs and arms on the foam pieces, as shown.

10 Cut away the unwanted sections.

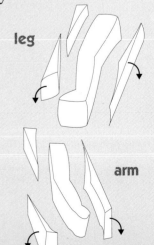

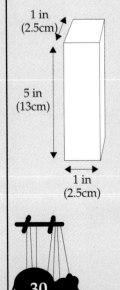

ASSEMBLY MATERIALS
dark thread
scissors
glue
string
two-legged control
   rod, p29
two chairs

TRAPEZE ARTIST ASSEMBLY

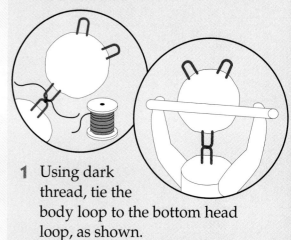

1 Using dark thread, tie the body loop to the bottom head loop, as shown.

2 Glue the hands to the ends of the trapeze bar, as shown.

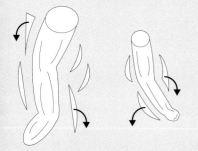

11 Trim the corners and edges with scissors to make the legs and arms rounded.

12 Attach the arms and legs to the body, using a glue gun or 5-minute epoxy. Remember to keep the loop on the body section at the top, as shown. Paint the body and the head. Shellac.

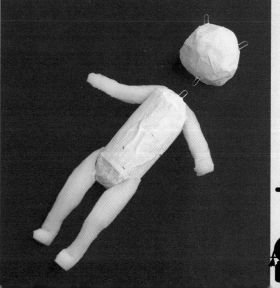

31

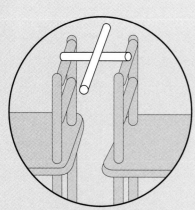

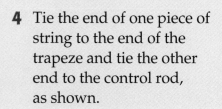

3 Set the two-legged control rod on the backs of two chairs, as shown. Measure a comfortable height for puppet player to work the marionette. Cut two pieces of string this length.

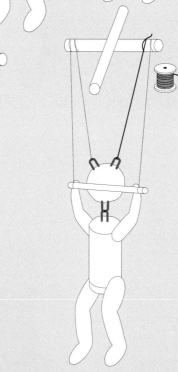

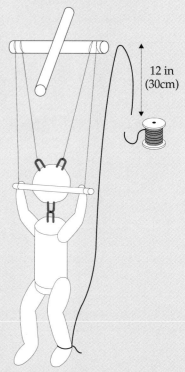

4 Tie the end of one piece of string to the end of the trapeze and tie the other end to the control rod, as shown.

5 Repeat on the other side of the control rod, as shown.

12 in (30cm)

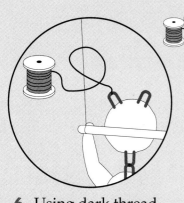

6 Using dark thread on a spool, tie the thread to one of the loops on the marionette head. Unwind enough thread to reach the control rod.

7 Wrap the thread around the same end of the rod as the string from the trapeze, as shown. Cut off the spool and tie.

8 Attach the thread to the other head loop in the same way. Attach to the control rod on the opposite side, as before.

9 Tie the thread from the spool around one foot of the marionette, and unwind enough thread to reach the control rod, allow extra thread, as shown, and cut off the spool.

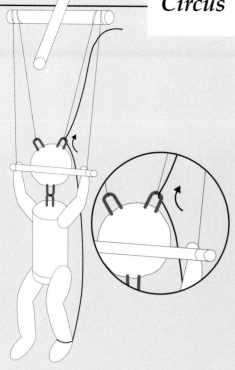

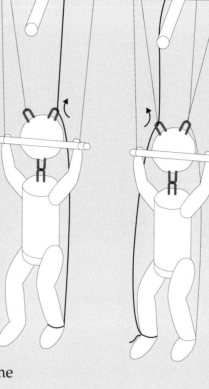

10 Pass the loose end of the thread behind the marionette and through the head loop on the same side as the leg, as shown. Take the thread up to the back of the control rod, wrap around the rod, and tie, as before. Repeat for the other leg, and attach to the same place on the control rod, as shown.

ELEPHANT

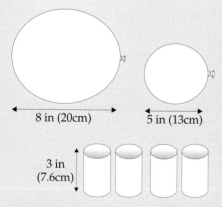

8 in (20cm)   5 in (13cm)

3 in (7.6cm)

1 Blow up two round balloons to the measurements shown, and set aside.

2 Cut four toilet tissue tubes, as shown.

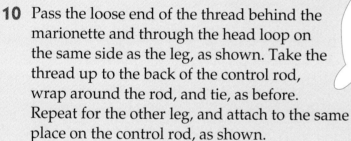

3 Place one tube on a sheet of thin cardboard and trace around it. Repeat making eight circles in all. Cut out and tape one circle over each end of each tube, as shown.

ELEPHANT MATERIALS
round balloons
toilet tissue tubes
thin cardboard
ruler
pencil
scissors
masking tape
glue
17 metal loops, p28
newspaper
wallpaper paste
paint
brushes
shellac
cushion foam
marker
utility knife
glue gun or
    5-minute epoxy
string

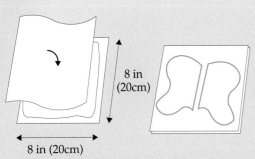

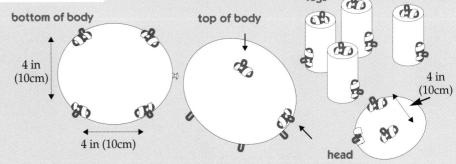

bottom of body

top of body

legs

4 in (10cm)

4 in (10cm)

4 in (10cm)

head

4 Cut two pieces of paper, as shown, and spread one piece with glue. Lay the other piece of paper on top of the glue and smooth in place.

5 Draw two elephant ears on this double sheet and cut out. Set aside.

8 in (20cm)

8 in (20cm)

6 Tape four metal loops to the bottom of the body balloon, as shown. Tape one loop on top in the center and tape another loop to one end of the balloon, as shown, to attach the head.

7 Tape one loop to the back of the head balloon and tape two loops to the top of the head, as shown.

8 Tape one loop to the top of each leg. Tape another loop to the side of each tube at the opposite end, as shown.

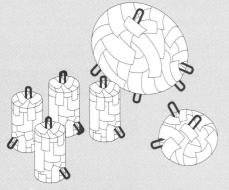

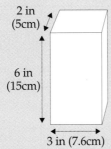

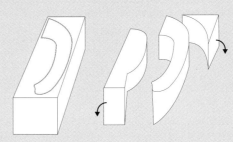

2 in (5cm)

6 in (15cm)

3 in (7.6cm)

9 Cover all the parts with strips of newspaper dipped in wallpaper paste. Do not cover the metal loops that stick up from the body parts, but make sure the loops are well attached to the body, as shown. Set aside to dry. Paint and shellac.

10 Cut a piece of foam and draw a curved elephant trunk, as shown.

11 Cut off the unwanted sections and trim the corners and edges with scissors to make the trunk rounded.

12 Cut horizontal snips in the foam, as

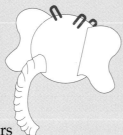

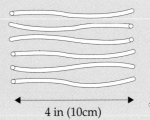

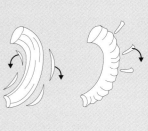

4 in (10cm)

13 Glue the ears to the head. Using a glue gun or 5-minute epoxy, glue the trunk to the head. Paint and shellac.

14 To make the tail, cut six pieces of string, as shown, and drizzle the pieces with glue. Twist together into a rope and paint.

15 Tape to hold the shape and attach to the body with glue. Tape in place until the glue dries.

ELEPHANT ASSEMBLY

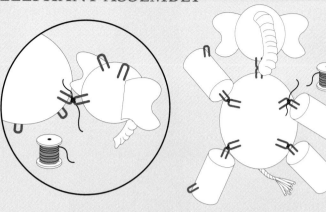

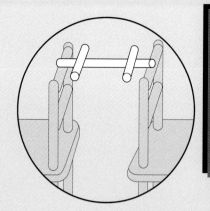

ASSEMBLY MATERIALS
dark thread
four-legged control
    rod, p29
2 chairs
scissors

1 Tie the loop on the front of the body to the loop on the back of the head using dark thread, as shown.

2 Tie each leg to the loops on the bottom of the body using dark thread.

3 Set the control rod across the backs of two chairs.

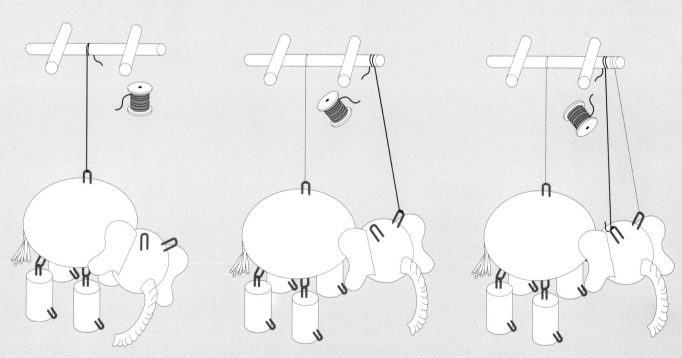

4 Tie dark thread to the loop on the elephant's back, as shown. Unwind enough thread to hang the elephant at a comfortable height for the puppet player from the control rod. Wrap the thread around the center of the control rod, cut off the spool, and tie the thread.

5 Tie the thread to one of the head loops. Unravel the thread and hang the head from the end of the control rod as shown. Secure thread, as before. Repeat for the other head loop, as shown.

6 To attach the legs to the rod, tie the thread to the loop on the side of one of the legs. Unwind the thread, and take it up to the control rod.

7 Wrap the thread around the end of the crosspiece above the same leg, as shown. Cut the thread and tie, as before. Attach the other legs in the same way, tying the thread from each leg to the end of the crosspiece above each leg, as shown.

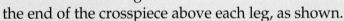

TRICK RIDER MARIONETTE MATERIALS
newspaper
ruler
pencil
scissors
masking tape
cardboard tube
5 metal loops, p28
cushion foam
marker
glue gun or
　5-minute epoxy
paint
brushes
shellac

TRICK RIDER

1 Make a marionette following the steps for the trapeze artist, pp30-31. Do not make the trapeze bar.

NOTE In Step 4, add one additional metal loop to the bottom of the body tube, as shown. This loop is used to attach the rider to the horse.

Step 4

body tube

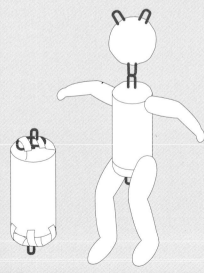

36

HORSE

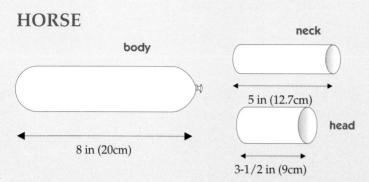

1 To make the body, blow up a long balloon to the measurement shown. Set aside.

2 To make the horse's head and neck, use two cardboard tubes, one larger in diameter than the other. The narrow tube is for the neck and the wider tube is for the head. Cut to the lengths shown.

HORSE MARIONETTE MATERIALS
oblong balloon
cardboard tubes
masking tape
pencil
scissors
paper
toilet tissue tubes
thin cardboard
19 metal loops, p28
newspaper strips
wallpaper paste
paint
brushes
shellac

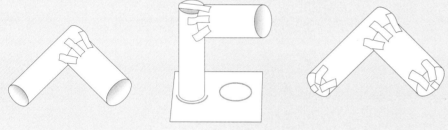

3 Place the tubes at a right angle and tape together, as shown.

4 Place the ends of the head and neck tubes on cardboard and trace around them. Cut out the circles.

5 Tape them over the open ends, as shown.

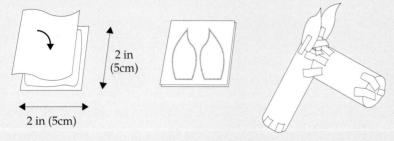

6 Cut two pieces of paper, as shown. Spread one piece of paper with glue. Lay the other piece of paper on top of the glue and smooth in place.

7 Draw two horse ears on the paper and cut out. Glue the ears to the horse's head. Set aside.

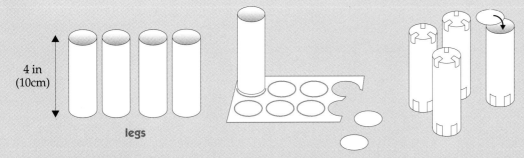

8 Collect four identical toilet tissue tubes, as shown.

9 Place one tube on a sheet of thin cardboard and trace around it. Repeat, drawing eight circles in all. Cut out the circles.

10 Tape a cardboard circle over each end of each tube.

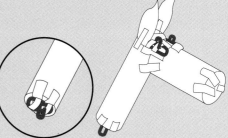

11 Tape four metal loops to the bottom of the body balloon for the legs, as shown.

12 Turn the body over and tape three loops to the top of the balloon to support the horse and to attach the rider. Tape one loop to the end of the balloon, as shown, to attach the neck.

13 Tape one loop to the bottom of the neck. Tape two loops to the head, as shown.

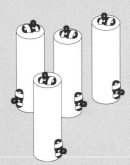

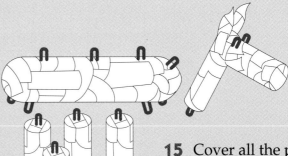

14 Tape one loop to the top of each leg. Tape another loop to the side of each tube at the opposite end, as shown.

15 Cover all the parts with strips of newspaper dipped in wallpaper paste. Do not cover the loops that stick up from the body parts, but make sure they are well attached to the body. Set aside to dry. Paint and shellac.

TRICK RIDER ASSEMBLY

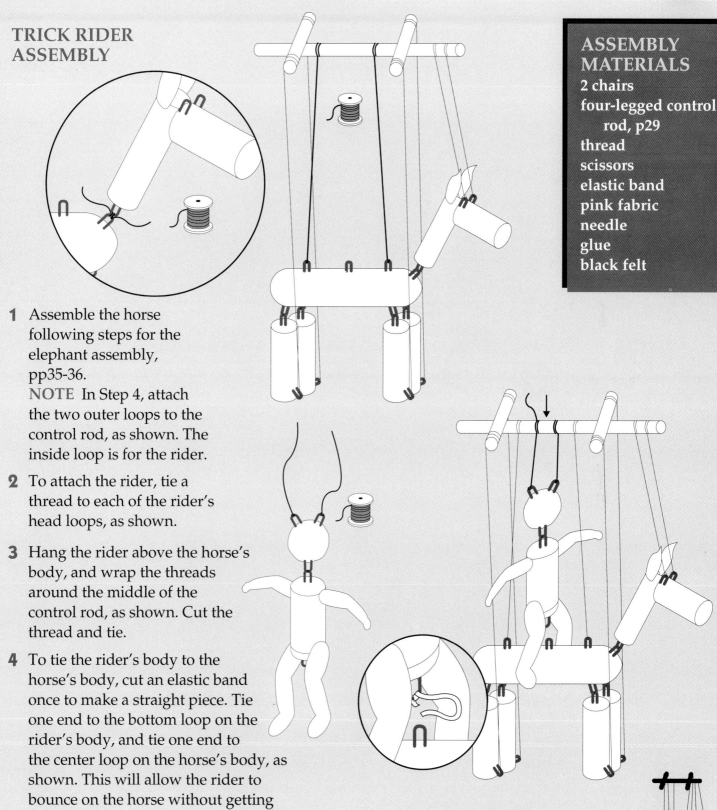

ASSEMBLY MATERIALS

2 chairs
four-legged control rod, p29
thread
scissors
elastic band
pink fabric
needle
glue
black felt

1 Assemble the horse following steps for the elephant assembly, pp35-36.
NOTE In Step 4, attach the two outer loops to the control rod, as shown. The inside loop is for the rider.

2 To attach the rider, tie a thread to each of the rider's head loops, as shown.

3 Hang the rider above the horse's body, and wrap the threads around the middle of the control rod, as shown. Cut the thread and tie.

4 To tie the rider's body to the horse's body, cut an elastic band once to make a straight piece. Tie one end to the bottom loop on the rider's body, and tie one end to the center loop on the horse's body, as shown. This will allow the rider to bounce on the horse without getting tangled in the strings.

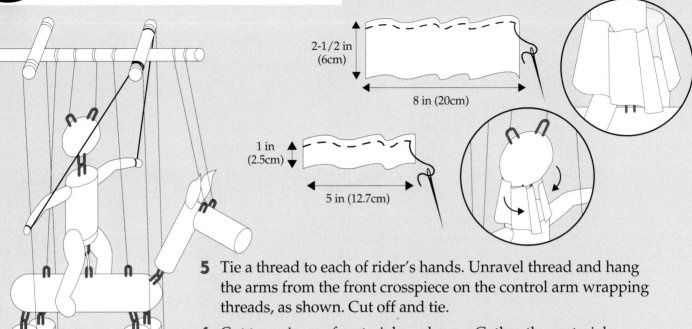

2-1/2 in (6cm)

8 in (20cm)

1 in (2.5cm)

5 in (12.7cm)

5 Tie a thread to each of rider's hands. Unravel thread and hang the arms from the front crosspiece on the control arm wrapping threads, as shown. Cut off and tie.

6 Cut two pieces of material, as shown. Gather the material slightly by stitching along one long side of each piece.

7 Wrap the larger piece of material around the rider's waist and glue in place, to hide the elastic. Wrap the smaller piece around the rider's neck and glue in place, to hide the metal loops.

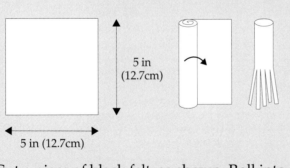

5 in (12.7cm)

5 in (12.7cm)

8 Cut a piece of black felt, as shown. Roll into a tube and glue. Make 2 in (5cm) cuts in one end. Glue this piece to the horse to make a tail, as shown.

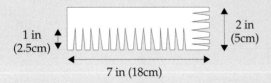

1 in (2.5cm)

2 in (5cm)

7 in (18cm)

9 Cut another piece of black felt, as shown. Make cuts in one end and along one long side, as shown. Glue to the horse's neck and head for a mane.

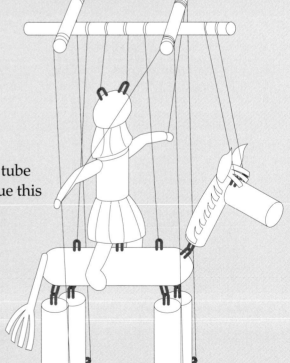

RUSH SEATS $.50

Make a Story

FRI. FEB 11   8:00 PM

FABRIC BOARD MATERIALS

cardboard
scissors
ruler
pencil
flannel fabric
masking tape
glue
ribbon or braid
rhinestones

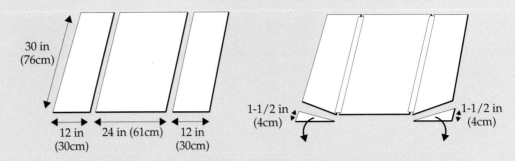

30 in (76cm)

12 in (30cm) 24 in (61cm) 12 in (30cm)

1-1/2 in (4cm) 1-1/2 in (4cm)

1 Cut three pieces of cardboard to the measurements shown. Tape the three pieces together to make one sheet 48 in (122cm) wide.

2 Cut a wedge out of each 12 in (30.5cm) side at the bottom, as shown.

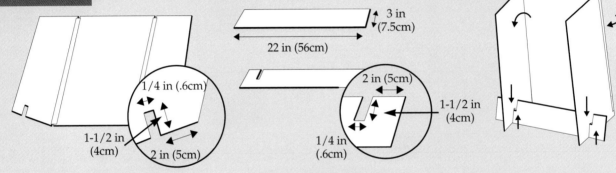

1/4 in (.6cm)

1-1/2 in (4cm)

2 in (5cm)

3 in (7.5cm)

22 in (56cm)

2 in (5cm)

1-1/2 in (4cm)

1/4 in (.6cm)

3 Cut a notch out of each angled corner from the end of the cardboard, as shown.

4 Cut another piece of cardboard, as shown. Cut a notch out of each end of this cardboard strip, as shown.

5 To make the fabric board stand up, fold back the two side sections and slide the cardboard strip notches into the side notches, as shown. Stand the sheet on edge with the cardboard strip at the bottom. The board will lean backward slightly, which helps to keep the felt figures in place.

6 Cut a piece of flannel fabric a little larger than the center section of the board, as shown.

Lay the fabric out flat and place the cardboard on top.

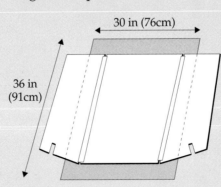

30 in (76cm)

36 in (91cm)

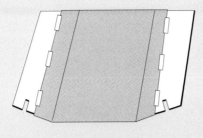

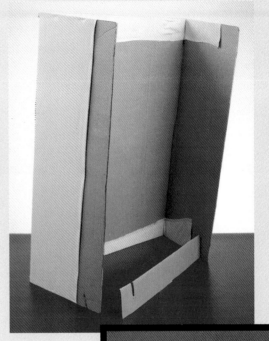

7 Fold the edges of the fabric over the top and bottom of the cardboard. Glue in place. Tape the cloth down until the glue dries.

8 Turn the board over. Glue and tape the fabric edges in place on the side sections of the cardboard. Do not cover the notches.

9 Set the board up again. Decorate the front section by gluing on ribbon or braid, and rhinestones, if desired. *See* photograph.

TO PERFORM

Set the fabric board on a table or the floor. Tell the story and add the felt characters to the board. Puppet players will enjoy moving and positioning the figures as the story progresses.

FELT CHARACTERS

Make felt figures to suit the characters in the story. Felt is available in many colors from fabric or hobby stores. Stiff white interfacing will also stick to the fabric board and can be colored with crayons or markers.

Story example The following patterns are given for characters in the story "There Was an Old Lady Who Swallowed a Fly."

Make a Story   felt characters

1 With a pencil, ruler, and piece of paper, draw a grid using the size of square given in the diagrams (*note the square size on each pattern diagram*). Copy the pattern diagram onto the paper grid a square at a time. Cut out the pattern. Using the color schemes, place the pattern on colored felt and cut out.

2 Cut out the individual parts for the characters and glue the pieces together using the placement guide on the diagram.

3 The characters can be detailed with fabric paint and glued on decorations.

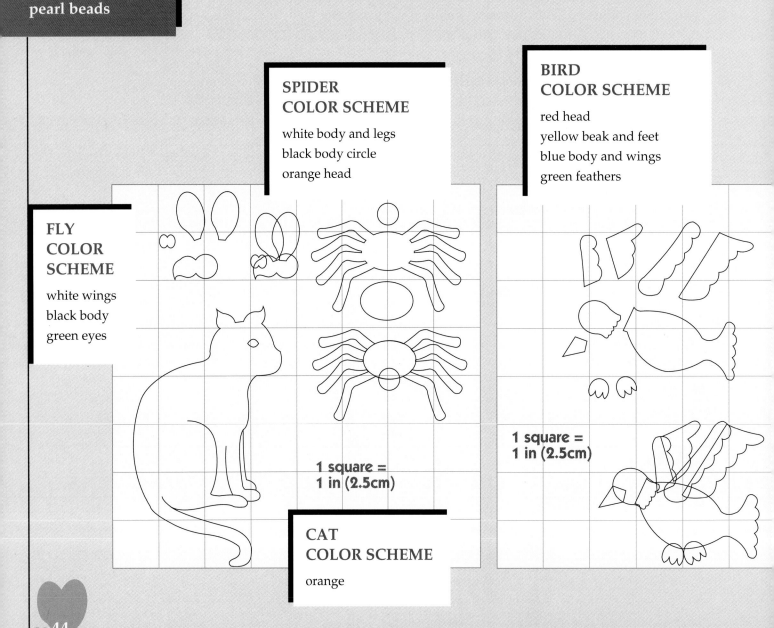

**SPIDER
COLOR SCHEME**

white body and legs
black body circle
orange head

**BIRD
COLOR SCHEME**

red head
yellow beak and feet
blue body and wings
green feathers

**FLY
COLOR
SCHEME**

white wings
black body
green eyes

1 square =
1 in (2.5cm)

1 square =
1 in (2.5cm)

**CAT
COLOR SCHEME**

orange

**DOG
COLOR SCHEME**

yellow

1 square = 2 in (5cm)

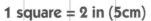

**HORSE
COLOR SCHEME**

red body
black tail, mane, forelock,
     hooves

**1 square =
3 in (7.6cm)**

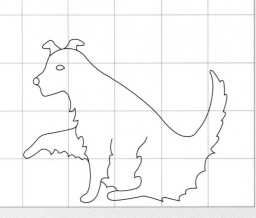

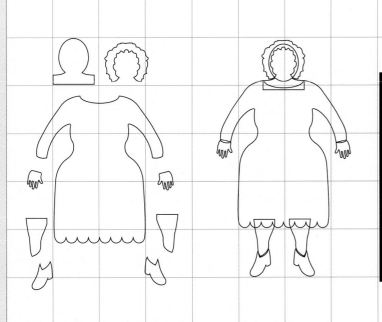

**LADY
COLOR SCHEME**

hot pink dress
beige head, legs, hands
black shoes
white hair and eyes
pink cheeks
red lips
pearl bead necklace

RUSH SEATS $.50

Down on the Farm

WED. SEPT 9   8:00 PM

Old
MacDonald's
Farm

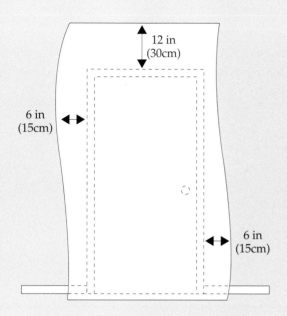

12 in
(30cm)

6 in
(15cm)

6 in
(15cm)

30 in
(76cm)

1 Measure the doorway and make a sheet of paper wider and higher than the door frame, as shown. Use a large sheet of paper or glue smaller sheets together to make one large sheet.

2 Choose a comfortable height for the puppet players to work the puppets. If that is 30 in (76cm), cut that amount from the bottom of the sheet.

3 Lay the paper on a flat surface (protect floor with plastic or newspaper.) Tape the paper to the floor cover and floor, if necessary. Paint the bottom sheet as the foreground (with the title of the play, grass, and flowers) and the top sheet as the background (a landscape in the distance). Shellac. *See* photo.

4 Tape the painted screens over the open doorway with masking tape. Place the bottom piece in front of the doorway facing the audience. Place the top piece behind the door, overlapping the bottom piece, as shown.

title of play

6 in
(15cm)

47

HOUSE

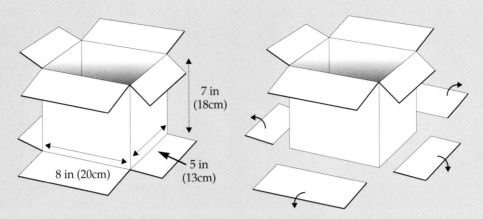

7 in (18cm)

8 in (20cm)

5 in (13cm)

1 For the house use a cardboard box, as shown. Open all the flaps on the box and cut off the flaps on the bottom, as shown.

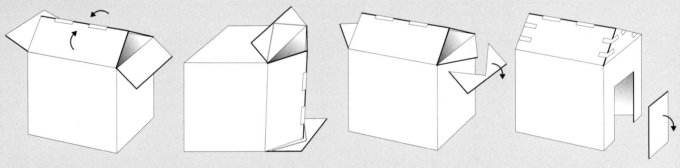

2 On the top of the box, bring the two long flaps together and tape, forming a roof, as shown.

3 Place the box on one end. Trace around the peak of the roof on the end flaps, as shown. Repeat for other end. Cut off the excess, as shown.

4 Tape in place. Cut out a doorway in one end of the house.

5 Cover the house with strips of newspaper covered with glue or wallpaper paste. One layer of paper is enough to cover the joins in the cardboard and the tape. When the papier-mâché is dry, paint the house. Shellac.

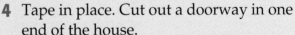

BARN

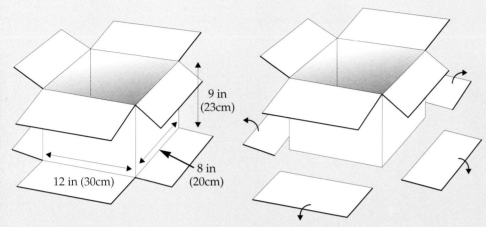

9 in (23cm)

12 in (30cm)

8 in (20cm)

1 For the barn use a cardboard box, as shown. Open all the flaps on the box and cut off the flaps on the bottom, as shown.

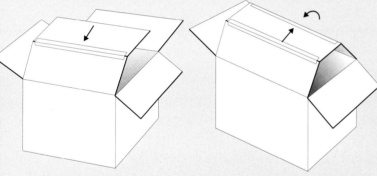

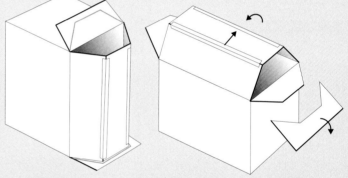

2 Tape one of the long flaps cut off the bottom to a long flap on the top of the box, as shown.

3 Bring up the other long flap and tape in place, forming a flat roof.

4 Place the box on end and trace around the roof on the end flaps, as shown. Cut off the excess, as shown.

5 Tape in place. Cut out a doorway in one end of the barn and fold the door pieces back, as shown.

6 Cover the barn with one layer of strips of newspaper covered with glue or wallpaper paste. When dry, paint the barn. Shellac.

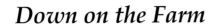

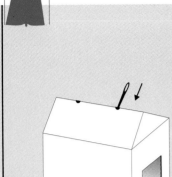

▲ 6 in
▼ (15cm)

1 To hang the buildings, poke two holes in the roof of each building.

2 Measure the distance from the top of the doorway to where the buildings should hang. Cut the string longer than what you measured, as shown, to make a knot. Cut two strings for each building.

3 Tie a large knot in the end of each string and thread one string through each hole in the roof of the building, as shown. Tape the strings to the top of the doorway. The buildings should hang just above the bottom doorway screen. *See* photo, p46.

FLOUR-SALT CLAY RECIPE

4 cups flour
1 cup salt
1-1/2 cups water

Mix all ingredients together in a large bowl. Knead until smooth. Add small quantities of flour or water to adjust the texture. It should be smooth enough to be molded (not crumbly) but not so wet that the clay slumps.

NOTE Molded clay pieces take several days to air dry. The pieces can be placed on foil-lined pans and baked in the oven at 150°F (65°C) for 4 to 6 hours.

CHICKEN

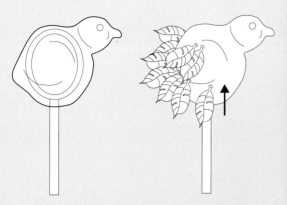

1 To make the chicken, model a clay body and head over the bowl of a wooden spoon, as shown.

2 While the clay is still soft, stick feathers into the clay. Start at the back of the bird, and work toward the head, overlapping the feathers, as shown.

3 Set aside to dry. Paint the head and the spoon handle with watercolor paints.

CHICKEN CLAY-AND-SPOON PUPPET MATERIALS
flour-salt clay
wooden spoon
feathers
watercolor paint
brushes

FARMER

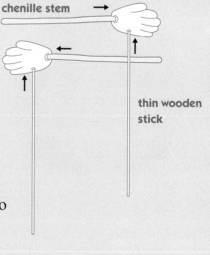

chenille stem →

thin wooden stick

1 Press a lump of clay over the bowl of a wooden spoon, as shown. Pinch and mold to form the farmer's head with a hat on top. Set aside to dry.

2 From small lumps of clay mold two hands.

3 Lay the hands on a flat surface facing in opposite directions, as shown. Press a chenille stem into the base of each hand, and a thin wooden stick into the bottom side of each hand, as shown. Allow to dry.

4 When all the clay pieces are dry paint the clay with watercolor paints.

FARMER CLAY-AND-SPOON PUPPET MATERIALS
flour-salt clay
wooden spoon
chenille stems
thin wooden sticks
watercolor paint
brushes
glue
paper
pencil
ruler
colored fabric

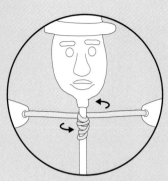

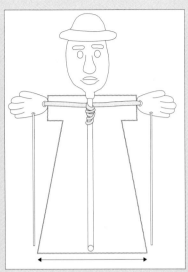

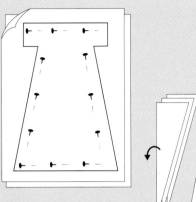

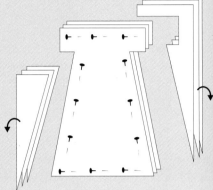

5 in (12.7cm)

5 Attach the hands to the wooden spoon by wrapping the ends of a chenille stem around the handle below the head, as shown. Hold in place with a drop of glue.

6 Lay the head and hands on paper to make a pattern for the farmer's clothing. Draw around the arms and the spoon handle. Leave enough space around the handle for the puppeteer's hand— at least 5 in (13cm).

7 Lay two pieces of colored cloth (one on top of another, wrong sides together) on a flat surface. Pin the paper pattern to the layers of cloth. Cut around the pattern, making two cloth shapes.

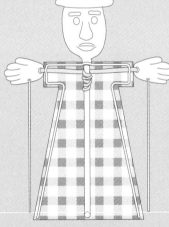

do not glue
this edge

8 Place one cloth shape right side down. Arrange the puppet head and arms on top of the cloth shape. Spread glue around the edges of the cloth, as shown.

9 Press the second cloth shape, right side up, to fit over the first cloth shape, covering the puppet. *Do not cover the thin wooden side sticks.* Allow to dry.

NOTE

Make additional puppets for the performance using the same basic technique described. Apply different shaped heads and hooves, and painted cloth bodies to create new characters for the play. *See* examples in the photograph, p53.

10 To work the clay-and-spoon puppets, hold the end of the wooden spoon handle with one hand. Hold the thin wooden sticks with the other hand. Lift and twirl the thin sticks to move the hands.

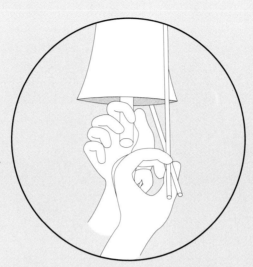

THEATER BOX MATERIALS

**cardboard box
ruler
pencil
scissors
paint
brushes
shellac
dark fabric
glue gun or velcro
glue
masking tape**

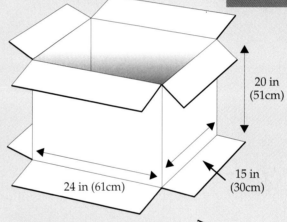

20 in (51cm)

24 in (61cm)

15 in (30cm)

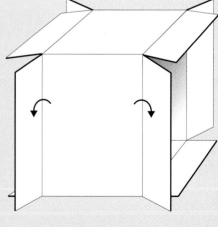

1 Select a cardboard box approximately the size shown. Open all the flaps.

2 Stand the box on one end. Fold the flaps on either side forward, as shown.

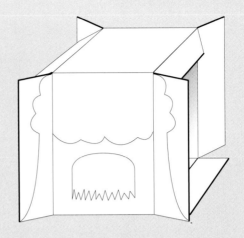

3 Draw a tree shape on each flap at the front of the box, and an opening in the center of the front, as shown.

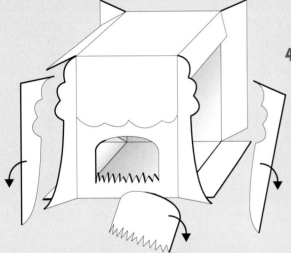

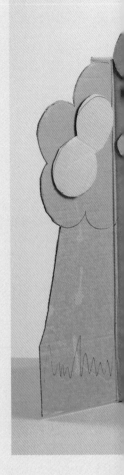

4 Cut out the opening in the front section, and cut off the excess cardboard from the tree side flaps, as shown. Put aside cardboard scraps.

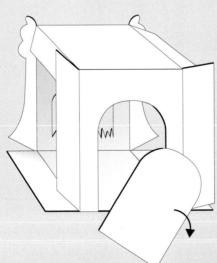

5 On the back of the theater, draw an opening to the bottom edge, as shown. This is for the puppet player to work through. Cut out the shape.

6 From the reserved cardboard scraps, cut out pieces of cardboard to represent branches and leaves. Glue the pieces to the front of the theater. *See* the photograph above. Paint the tree. When dry, shellac.

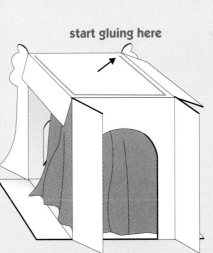

start gluing here

9 Tape the uncut side flaps closed to hold the box shape, as shown.

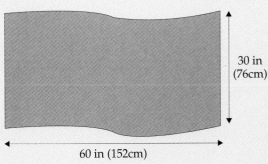

30 in (76cm)

60 in (152cm)

7 Cut a piece of dark fabric, as shown. The fabric must be large enough to wrap around the back and both sides of the theater. Hem the edges of the cloth, if desired.

8 Glue the cloth to the inside of the box, to cover the back and two sides. A glue gun works well for this, or use pieces of velcro glued to the inside of the box and the cloth. When attaching the cloth, start at one front top corner, as shown, and attach it around the top of the box. Distribute the extra length across the back of the theater so that the cloth is not tight across the back opening, as shown.

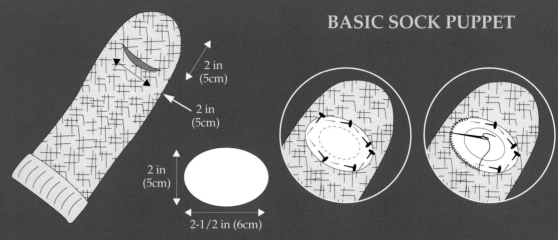

BASIC SOCK PUPPET

BASIC SOCK PUPPET MATERIALS

sock
ruler
scissors
pink felt
straight pins
needle
thread

2 in (5cm)

2 in (5cm)

2 in (5cm)

2-1/2 in (6cm)

1 Make a straight cut across the sock, as shown.

2 Cut out an oval mouth shape from pink felt, as shown.

3 Pin the felt shape over the cut in the sock. The sock material will stretch to fit around the felt.

4 Hand-sew the mouth to the sock, using pink thread to match the felt.

FROGGIE SOCK PUPPET MATERIALS

basic green sock
    puppet,58
black, white, red
    felt
ruler
scissors
straight pins
needle
black, white
    thread
glue
empty thread
    spool
button
eyes

FROGGIE

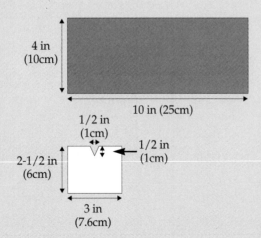

4 in (10cm)

10 in (25cm)

1/2 in (1cm)

1/2 in (1cm)

2-1/2 in (6cm)

3 in (7.6cm)

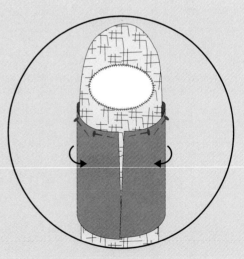

1 To make Froggie's suit, cut a piece of black felt and a piece of white felt, as shown. Cut a notch out of the middle of the white felt, as shown.

2 Wrap the black felt around the middle of the basic green sock puppet and pin it in place around the top edge.

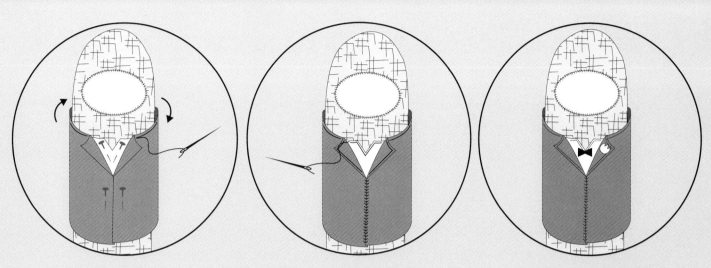

3 Fold back the top corners of the black felt to form lapels, and pin. Place the white felt under the front of the black felt, as shown, and pin in place. Sew the black felt in place by stitching around the top with black thread.

4 Sew the two ends of the black felt together down the middle, and sew the lapels in place. With white thread, sew the white felt shirt in place.

5 Cut out a black bow tie and red rose for froggie's lapel from scraps of felt. Glue in place.

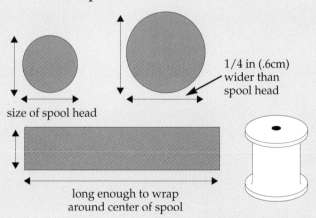

size of spool head

1/4 in (.6cm) wider than spool head

long enough to wrap around center of spool

6 To make a top hat, measure the spool you are using and cut out black felt to fit the parts shown. Glue one end of the black felt strip to the spool center, wrap around the spool and cut to fit. Glue the loose end of the strip down on the spool. Glue the largest circle of black felt to one end of the spool to create a hat brim. Finally, glue the small circle of felt to the remaining end of the spool.

7 Glue the top hat to Froggie's head. Sew a button on Froggie's jacket. Glue on two eyes. *See* photograph, p61.

MISS MOUSIE

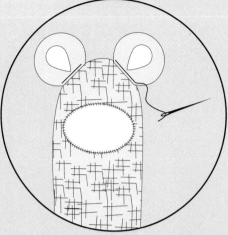

**MISS MOUSIE
SOCK PUPPET
MATERIALS**
basic gray sock
    puppet, p58
gray, white, pink
    felt
needle
gray thread
pink chenille stem
ruler
scissors
button
eyes

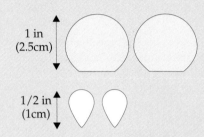

1 in (2.5cm)

1/2 in (1cm)

1 Cut out two ears shapes from gray felt and two teardrop shapes from pink felt, as shown.

2 Glue a pink shape to the center of each gray ear and sew the ears to the top of the basic gray sock puppet.

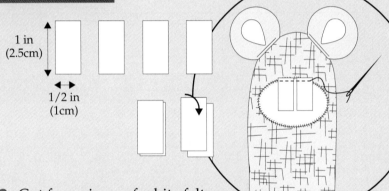

1 in (2.5cm)

1/2 in (1cm)

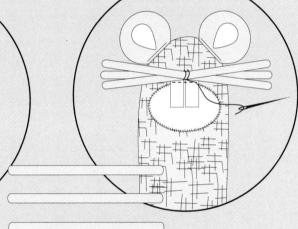

3 in (7.6cm)

3 Cut four pieces of white felt, as shown, and glue two pieces together to form a tooth. Repeat to make a second tooth. Sew the teeth to the top of the mouth, as shown.

4 Cut the chenille stem into three pieces, as shown.

5 Sew these above the teeth to form whiskers, as shown.

6 Sew a black button on top of the whiskers for a nose. Glue on two eyes.

7 To make a wedding dress, cut a piece of lace trim 6 in (15cm) wide and 20 in (50cm) long. Gather the lace along one long side, and sew in place around Miss Mousie's neck.

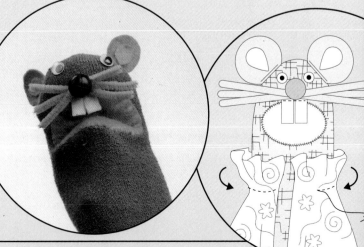

60

UNCLE RAT

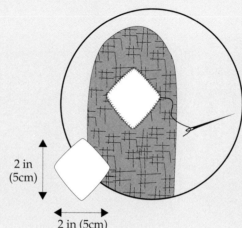

2 in
(5cm)

2 in (5cm)

**UNCLE RAT
SOCK PUPPET
MATERIALS**
black sock
black, pink, hot pink,
   blue, white felt
ruler
scissors
black chenille stem
button
eyes
glue
needle
black, white, pink ,
   hot pink thread

1 To give Uncle Rat a pointy snout, cut the hot pink mouth shape in a diamond instead of a circle in the basic sock puppet instructions, p58.

2 Sew the diamond shape in place with hot pink thread, with a corner at the top and bottom of the opening, as shown.

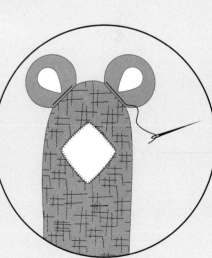

1 in
(2.5cm)

1/2 in
(1cm)

3 Cut out two ear shapes from black felt, and two teardrop shapes from pink felt, as shown.

4 Glue a pink shape to the center of each black ear and sew the ears to the top of the sock with black thread.

Froggie Goes A'Courtin'   Uncle Rat

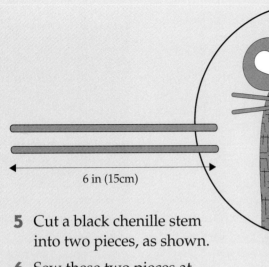

6 in (15cm)

5 Cut a black chenille stem into two pieces, as shown.

6 Sew these two pieces at the top of the mouth, as shown, to form whiskers.

7 Sew a large black button on top of the whiskers for a nose. Glue on two eyes.

8 Cut a piece of white felt, as shown, for a collar.

9 Wrap the felt around the neck area and pin in place. Fold the ends back at the center and cut at an angle, as shown. Pin in place.

10 With white thread, sew the collar to the sock all around the top edge of the felt, and sew the folded ends of the felt together. Sew the collar points down.

11 Cut out a necktie shape from blue felt. Glue it underneath the collar, *see* photo, p61.

1 in (2.5cm)

9 in (23cm)

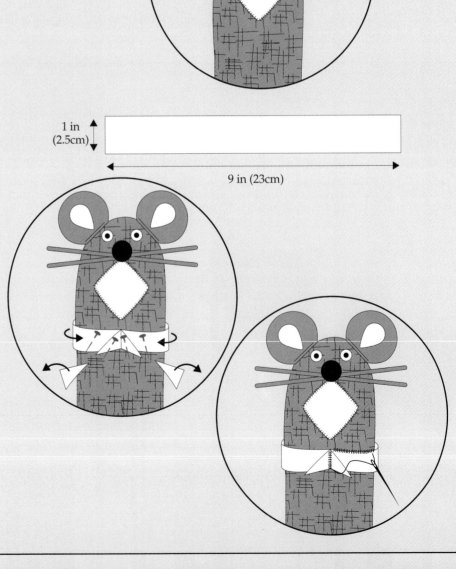

RUSH SEATS   **$.50**

Outer Space

MON. JAN 7   **8:00 PM**

Outer Space doorway screens

DOORWAY SCREEN MATERIALS

dark blue, green, brown fabric

ruler

scissors

needle

dark blue, green, brown thread

rhinestones

glitter

colored felt

glue

table

straight pins

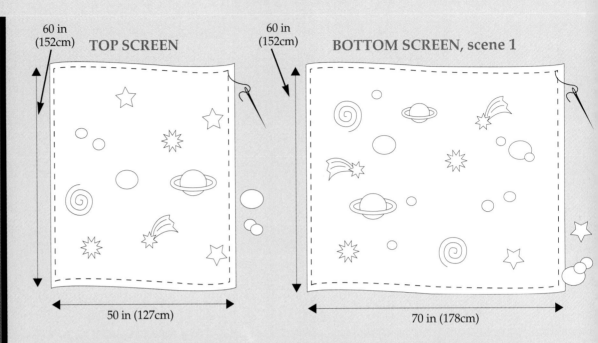

60 in (152cm) — TOP SCREEN — 50 in (127cm)

60 in (152cm) — BOTTOM SCREEN, scene 1 — 70 in (178cm)

1 For the top screen, cut dark blue fabric, as shown. Hem all edges to prevent unraveling. Glue rhinestones to the fabric for stars. Cut out planets and comets from colored felt and sew or glue to the fabric.

2 For the bottom screen, scene 1—deep space—cut the same blue fabric to the measurements shown. Hem and decorate this screen in the same way as the first.

3 For the bottom screen, scene 2—Venus with its greenish atmosphere—cut green fabric to the measurements shown. Hem all edges, as before. Cut a semi-circle from brown fabric and pin the semi-circle along the bottom edge, as shown. Stitch in place.

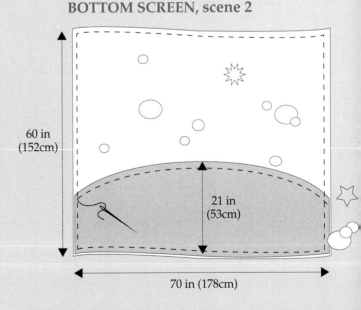

BOTTOM SCREEN, scene 2

60 in (152cm)

21 in (53cm)

70 in (178cm)

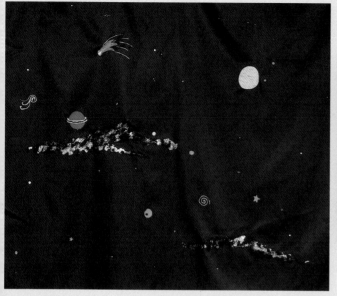

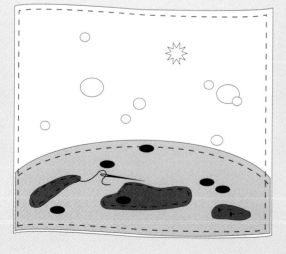

4 Add other scrap pieces of fabric to the planet to create a landscape. Pin in place and stitch. Glue on dark craters of felt or sparkles, as desired. Add stars to the sky area.

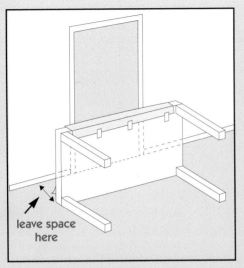

leave space here

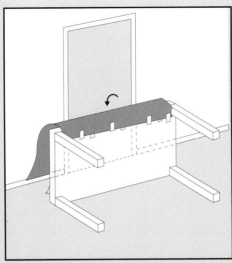

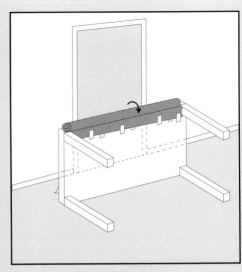

1 Lay a rectangular table on its side behind a doorway, as shown, leaving enough space for the puppets to exit and enter the stage. Drape bottom screen, scene 1 over the table and tape it to the back of the table, as shown.

2 Drape bottom screen, scene 2 over the table, overtop scene 1. Tape in place in the same way.

3 Roll up scene 2 from the front and lay across the legs behind the table, as shown.

TO PERFORM

The puppet player stands behind the table and works the marionettes in front of the table. The table is far enough away from the wall and doorway to allow the puppets to enter and exit in front of the table. To change the scene, unroll scene 2 and let it fall in front of scene 1.

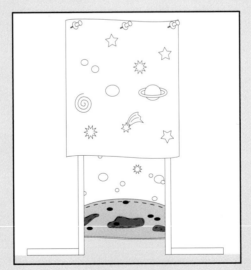

4 Pin or tape the top screen across the front of the doorway, overlapping the bottom screen about 6 in (15cm). To change the scene, unroll scene 2 and let it fall in front of scene 1.

SPACE STATION

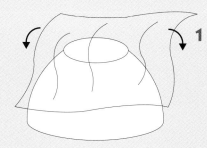

1 To make the center dome, place a mixing bowl upside down and cover with plastic wrap. Set aside.

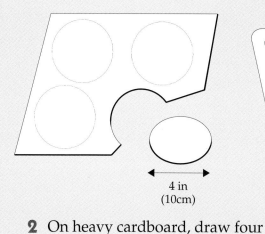

4 in
(10cm)

2 On heavy cardboard, draw four circles, as shown, and cut out.

3 Cut the cups off an egg carton and tape three egg cups to each cardboard circle, as shown. Set aside.

8 in
(20cm)

8 in (20cm)

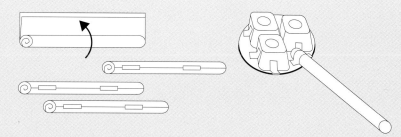

4 Use a section of newspaper that is three or four sheets folded together. Cut into four pieces, as shown.

5 Roll each square into a tight tube, and tape to secure.

6 Glue and tape one newspaper tube to each cardboard circle, as shown.

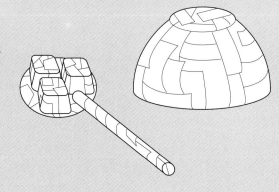

7 Cover the mixing bowl with strips of newspaper dipped in wallpaper paste. Cover the cardboard circles and tubes with newspaper strips and paste, as well.

8 Set the bowl in the middle of the work surface. Arrange the cardboard circles around the bowl, as shown. Attach the ends of the tubes to the center dome with strips of newspaper and wallpaper paste. Use several layers of paper to make the joins strong, *see* detail.

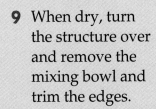

9 When dry, turn the structure over and remove the mixing bowl and trim the edges.

10 Place the central dome on cardboard and trace around it.

11 Cut out the circle and glue to the dome.

SPACE STATION ASSEMBLY

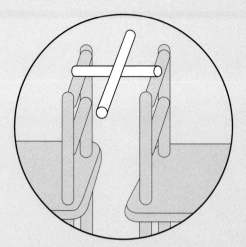

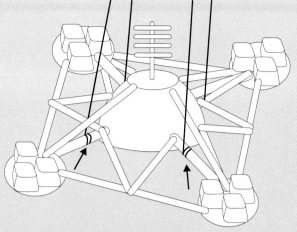

ASSEMBLY MATERIALS
two-legged control
  rod, p29
2 chairs
scissors
dark thread

1 Set the control rod across the backs of two chairs, as shown.

2 Measure a comfortable height for the puppet player to hold the marionette. Mark a piece of string this length, adding extra to wrap around the control rod. Cut four pieces this length. Tie the thread to the space station at strong places on the structure, as shown. Hang the station from the control rod so that it is balanced and level.

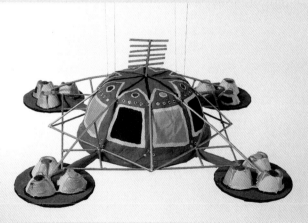

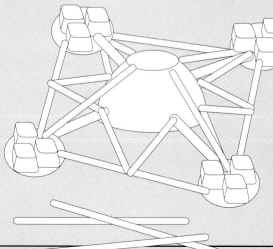

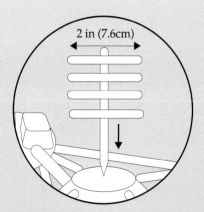

2 in (7.6cm)

12 Glue thin wooden sticks around the structure, connecting the "pods" to the dome and to each other. When the glue is dry, paint and shellac.

13 Make an antennae using pieces of thin wooden sticks, as shown, and push it into the top of the dome. Glue in place.

SPACESHIP

SPACESHIP MARIONETTE MATERIALS

cardboard tube
ruler
pencil
scissors
masking tape
thin cardboard
4 metal loops, p28
newspaper strips
wallpaper paste
paint
brushes
shellac

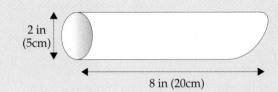

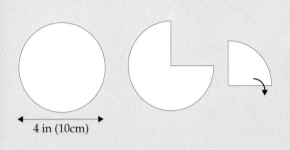

2 in (5cm)

8 in (20cm)

4 in (10cm)

1 Cut a cardboard tube to the measurements shown cutting one end at an angle.

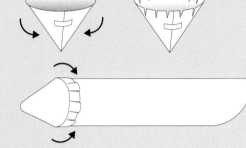

2 Cut out one circle of paper, as shown. Cut out a quarter section, as shown.

3 Overlap the cut edges to make a cone and tape. Make cuts all around the edge of the cone, as shown.

4 Place the cone over the straight end, as shown. Fold the tabs down onto the tube and tape in place.

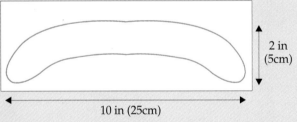

2 in (5cm)

10 in (25cm)

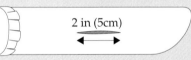

2 in (5cm)

5 On thin cardboard draw a wing shape, as shown, and cut out.

6 Make a cut through both sides of the tube; as shown.

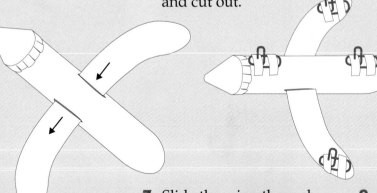

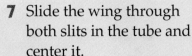

7 Slide the wing through both slits in the tube and center it.

8 Tape one metal loop to the top of each wing near the wing tip, as shown. Tape two loops on top of the body, as shown.

SPACESHIP ASSEMBLY

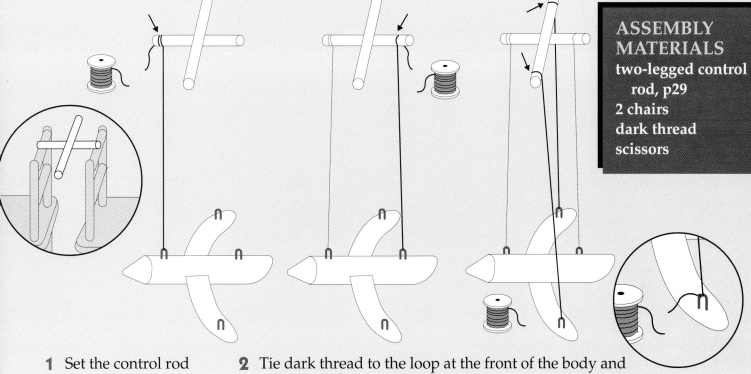

ASSEMBLY MATERIALS
two-legged control
  rod, p29
2 chairs
dark thread
scissors

1 Set the control rod across the back of two chairs, as shown.

2 Tie dark thread to the loop at the front of the body and unwind enough thread to hang the plane from the control rod at a comfortable height for the puppet player to operate the marionette. Wrap the thread around one end of the control rod, cut off the thread, and tie, as shown.

3 Tie thread to the loop at the back of the body. Attach this thread to the opposite end of the control rod, adjusting the thread length so the plane hangs level.

4 Tie a thread to each loop on each wing and unwind enough thread to the control arm above each wing, as shown. Wrap, cut off, and tie, as before.

9 Cover the plane with strips of newspaper dipped in wallpaper paste. Do not cover the loops that stick up from the plane. Do not cover the open end of the tube. Allow to dry. Paint and shellac.

TRANSPARENT SPACE MONSTER MARIONETTE MATERIALS

newspaper
ruler
masking tape
1 metal loops, p28
wallpaper paste
thin wooden sticks
3 chenille stems
scissors
plasticine
paint
brushes
shellac
round balloon
straw
glitter

TRANSPARENT SPACE MONSTER

2 in (5cm)

1 Crumple a sheet of newspaper into a ball for the head, as shown. Tape to hold the shape.

2 Tape a metal loop to the ball, as shown.

3 Cover the ball with strips of newspaper dipped in wallpaper paste. Set aside to dry.

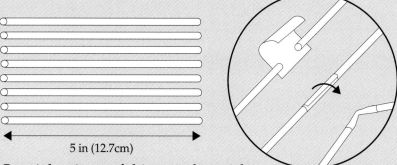

5 in (12.7cm)

4 Cut eight pieces of thin wooden sticks for the legs, as shown.

5 Join two sticks by wrapping masking tape around two ends, as shown. The masking tape will bend in the middle like a knee.

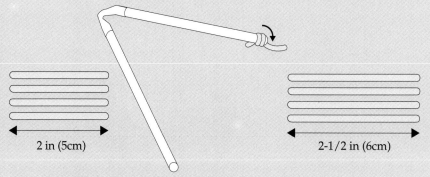

2 in (5cm)   2-1/2 in (6cm)

6 Cut a chenille stem into four pieces, as shown.

7 Wrap 1 in (2.5cm) of stem around the end of each leg, leaving 1 in (2.5cm) unwound, as shown. Glue in place.

8 Cut four longer pieces of chenille stem, as shown.

9 Attach these pieces to the other end of each leg. Wrap a 1/2 in (1.3cm) ball of plasticine around the end of the leg and the middle of the chenille stem, as shown.

10 Bend each chenille stem into a hook, as shown. This is a foot.

11 Paint the head and the wooden legs, and shellac.

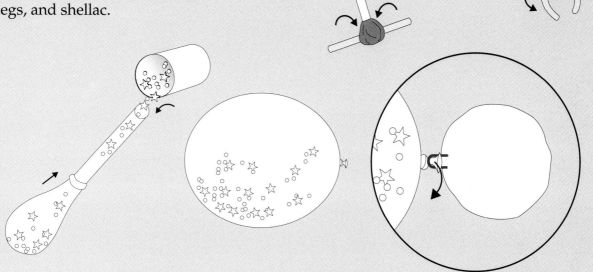

12 To make the body, pull the opening of a clear balloon over the end of a straw, and pour glitter through the straw into the balloon. Remove the straw.

13 Very carefully blow up the balloon and tie the opening closed. *Do not inhale air out of the balloon or you may inhale glitter.*

14 Push the balloon knot through the loop on the head, as shown.

15 Wrap a chenille stem around the neck to hide the loop and knot, as shown.

16 Wrap the chenille stem at the top of each leg around the same neck area.

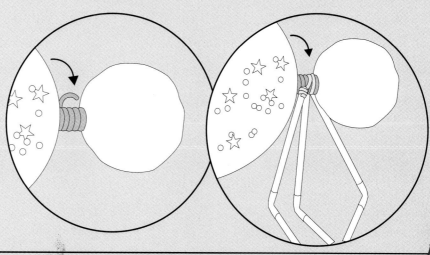

ASSEMBLY
MATERIALS
two-legged control
    rod, p29
2 chairs
dark thread
scissors

TRANSPARENT SPACE MONSTER ASSEMBLY

1 Set the control rod across the backs of two chairs, as shown.

2 String the marionette using dark thread. Tie thread around the neck, and unwind enough thread to hang the marionette at a comfortable height from the control rod. Wrap thread around the control rod. Cut off and tie, as shown.

3 Tie a thread around each "knee" and unwind each thread to the control rod, as shown. Wrap threads around the control rod. Cut off and tie, as shown.

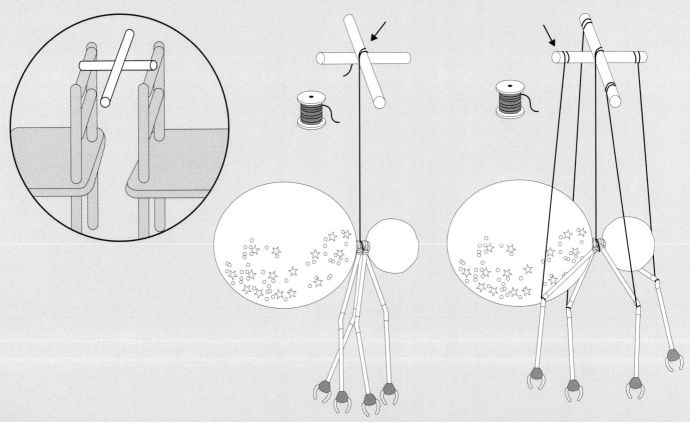

2-HEADED SPACE MONSTER

1 To make the body, crumple newspaper together to make a flattened ball, as shown. Tape to hold the shape. Set aside.

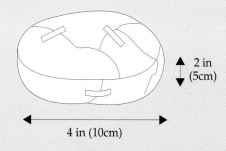

2 in (5cm)

4 in (10cm)

1-1/2 in (4cm)

2 Cut toilet tissue tubes into eight pieces, as shown.

2-HEADED SPACE MONSTER MARIONETTE MATERIALS
cardboard tube
ruler
scissors
masking tape
thin cardboard
pencil
19 metal loops, p28
newspaper strips
wallpaper paste
paint
brushes
shellac

3 Place one tube on thin cardboard and trace around it. Repeat, making sixteen circles. Cut out the circles.

4 Tape a cardboard circle over each end of each tube.

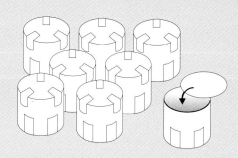

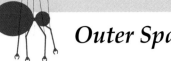
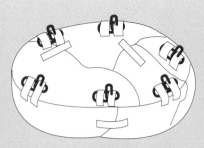

bottom of body

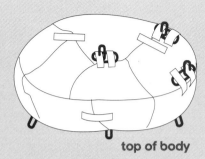

top of body

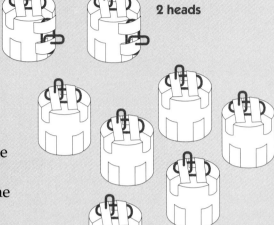

2 heads

6 feet

5 Tape six metal loops to the bottom of the body ball to attach legs, as shown.

6 Tape one loop to the top of the body ball. Tape two loops on the top, as shown, to attach the heads.

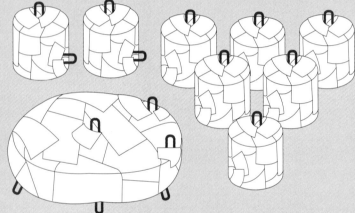

7 Use two of the cardboard tubes for heads. Tape one loop to the end of each tube and tape one loop to the side, as shown.

8 Tape one loop to the end of the remaining six tubes for feet.

9 Cover all the parts with strips of newspaper dipped in wallpaper paste. Do not cover the loops that stick up from the body parts, but make sure they are well attached to the body. Set aside to dry. Paint all the parts.

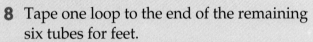

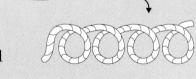

10 Paint a face on the ends of the heads without a loop, as shown, and shellac.

11 Cut two different colored chenille stems, 12 in (30cm) long for the necks. Put one stem of each color together and twist together, as shown.

12 Wrap around your finger, as shown, and slide the stem off your finger, making a corkscrew shape. This is one neck. Make another neck in the same way.

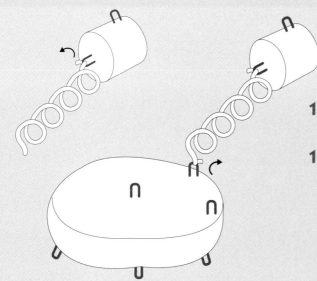

13 Wrap one end of the corkscrew neck around the loop at the end of one head.

14 Wrap the other end around one of the side loops on the body, as shown. Attach the other head in the same way.

15 Cut six chenille stems, as shown, for legs.

16 Hook one stem through the loop of each foot and hook the other end of the chenille stem through a body loop, as shown.

6 in (15cm)

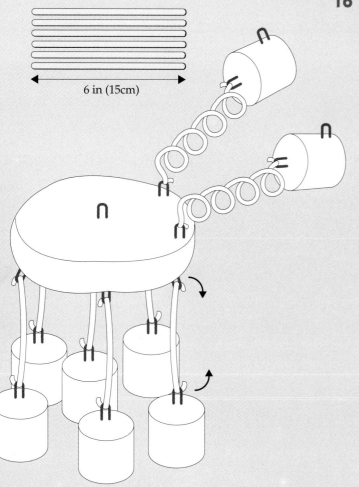

2-HEADED SPACE MONSTER ASSEMBLY

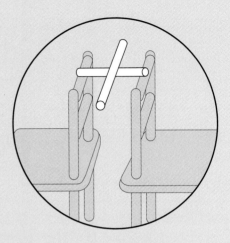

1 Set the control rod across the back of two chairs, as shown.

2 Tie a thread to the loop on the center of the body, as shown, and unwind enough thread to hang the marionette at a comfortable height from the control rod. Wrap the thread around the center of the control rod. Cut off and tie.

3 Tie thread to the side loop of one head.

4 Hang the head from one arm of the control rod, near the middle, as shown. Wrap the thread around the rod. Cut off and tie. Attach the other head to the other control rod arm, as shown.

ASSEMBLY MATERIALS
two-legged control rod, p29
2 chairs
dark thread
scissors

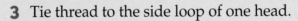

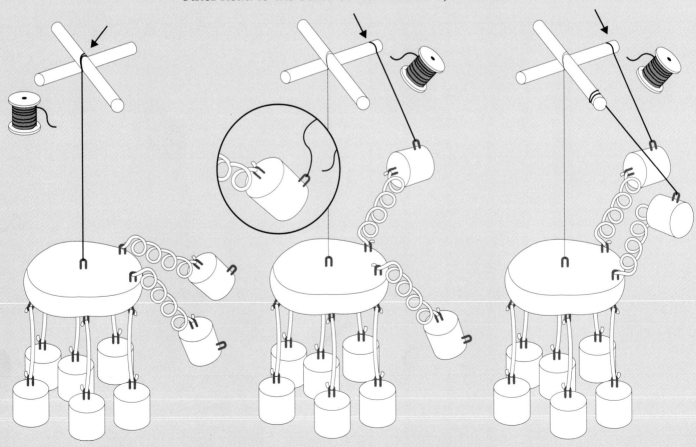

5 Tie thread to the loop on top of one leg, as shown, and unwind enough thread to reach the control rod. Wrap the thread near the end of one of the control rods, as shown.

6 There are more legs on the monster than arms on the control rod. Attach two legs to the control rod arms that do not have a head tied to them, as shown.

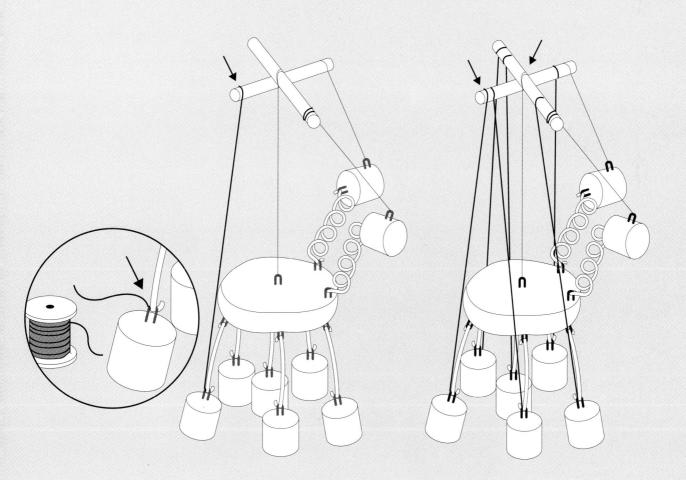

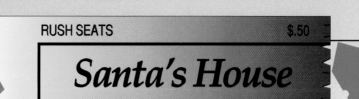

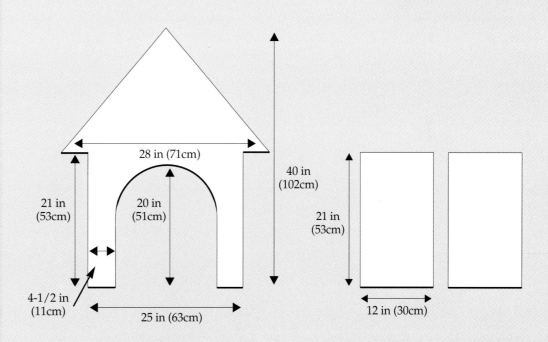

28 in (71cm)

40 in (102cm)

21 in (53cm)

20 in (51cm)

21 in (53cm)

4-1/2 in (11cm)

25 in (63cm)

12 in (30cm)

1 From a large cardboard box, cut a basic house shape, as shown.

2 Cut two smaller pieces for the side walls (wings) of the house. Lay the pieces flat.

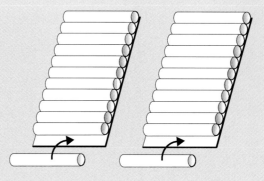

3 Cut cardboard tubes 12 in (30cm) long and cover the wings, as shown. Glue in place.

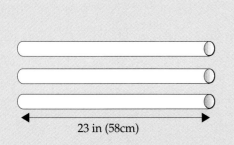

23 in (58cm)

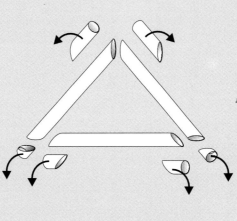

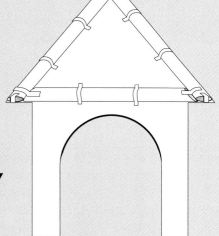

4 Cut three more cardboard tubes, as shown. Use these tubes to outline the triangle of the roof shape. Cut the ends of the tubes at an angle and fit them together, as shown. Glue and tape in place on the roof triangle, as shown.

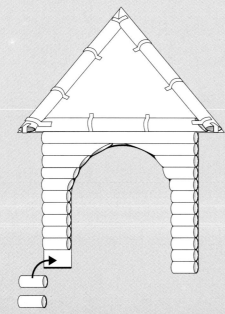

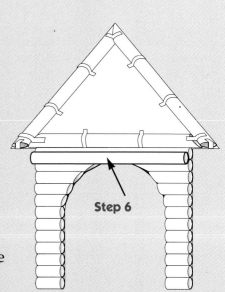

Step 6

5 Cut more tubes to cover the bottom front of house, as shown.

6 Glue another 25 in (64cm) long cardboard tube above the doorway, as shown.

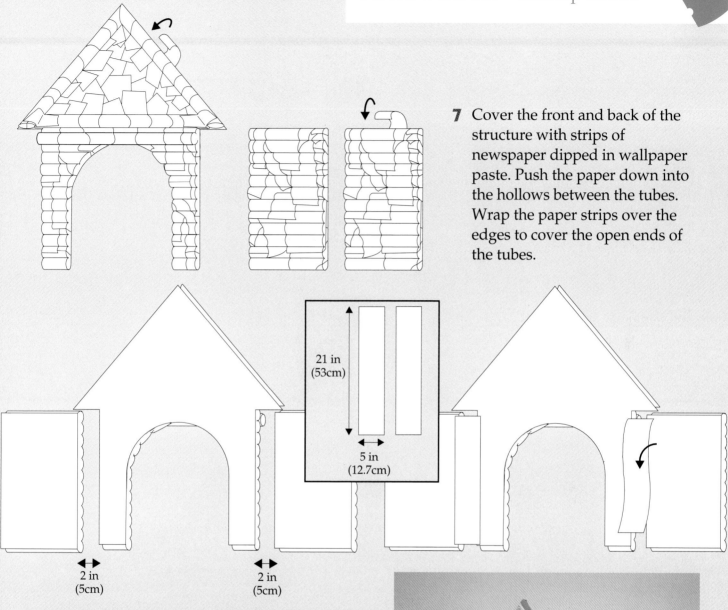

7 Cover the front and back of the structure with strips of newspaper dipped in wallpaper paste. Push the paper down into the hollows between the tubes. Wrap the paper strips over the edges to cover the open ends of the tubes.

21 in
(53cm)

5 in
(12.7cm)

2 in
(5cm)

2 in
(5cm)

8 Arrange the three pieces side by side, as shown, with the smooth side up. Place the largest piece in the middle, as shown.

9 Cut two pieces of paper, as shown.

10 Spread each strip of paper with glue and use them to join the side wall to the center wall, as shown. When dry, stand the theater up. The paper strips act as hinges, letting the wings fold backwards or forwards.

11 Paint the tube side to resemble a log cabin. Paint the smooth side to resemble a home. Shellac.

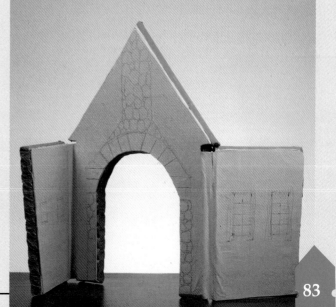

83

Santa's House   paper bag puppets

TO PERFORM

Place the theater on a tabletop with either scene forward. The wings of the scene being used should be facing forward. The puppet players may stand behind and/or in front of the table with the puppets as they act out the story.

PAPER BAG PUPPETS

1 Lay one brown bag flat, open end at the top.

2 Spread glue inside the fold along each side of the bag. Press closed. Spread glue under the folded bottom of the bag and press closed, as shown.

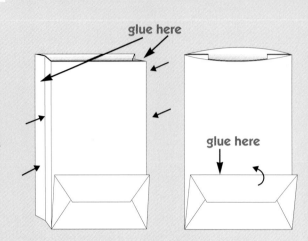

glue here

glue here

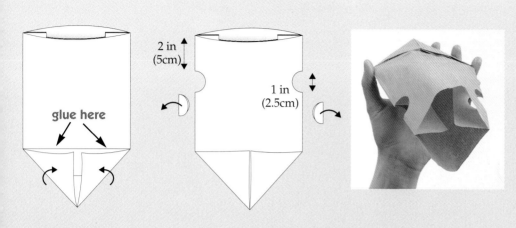

glue here

2 in
(5cm)

1 in
(2.5cm)

3 Fold the bottom corners into the center, as shown, and glue in place.

4 Cut a half circle out of each side of the bag, as shown, for the puppet player's thumb and little finger. Paint the bag as desired and shellac. *See* photo below for suggestions.

**SHADOW BOX
THEATER
MATERIALS**
large cardboard box
scissors
ruler
pencil
masking tape
glue
paint
brushes
shellac
white paper
100 watt lightbulb
    in a lamp

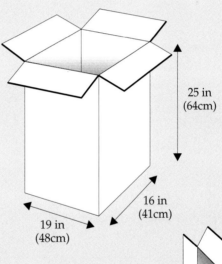

25 in
(64cm)

16 in
(41cm)

19 in
(48cm)

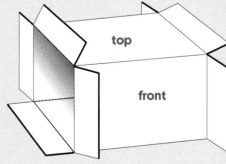

top

front

1 Select a cardboard box similar to the
measurements given above. Turn the
box on its side and open up the flaps
at both ends. Choose a front side and
mark it.

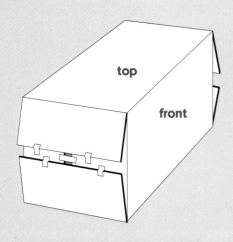

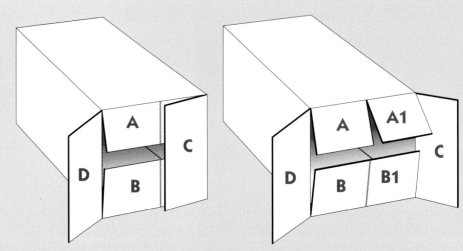

2 Tape one end of the box shut to hold its shape as you work on it.

3 At the opposite end, mark the flaps, as shown. Arrange the flaps so that flaps A and B are on the inside, and flap C is on top, as shown. Mark along the edge of flap C on flaps A and B, as shown.

4 Fold back flap C, and cut along both drawn lines, making flaps A, A1, and B, B1.

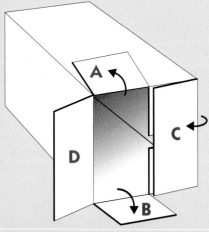

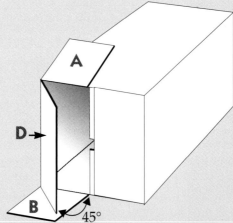

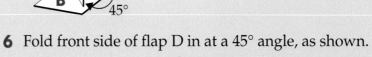

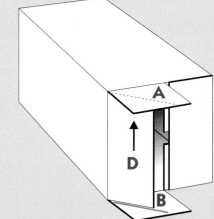

5 Fold flap C back against flaps A1 and B1 and glue in place, as shown. Fold flaps A and B, as shown.

6 Fold front side of flap D in at a 45° angle, as shown.

7 Rest flap A on the top edge of flap D and draw a line along the edge of flap D on flaps A and B, as shown.

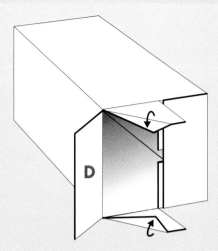

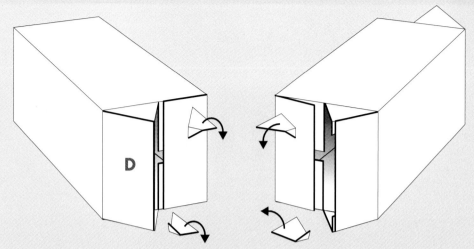

8 Fold back flap D.

9 Fold flaps A and B along drawn lines, as shown.

10 Glue flap D against the folded corners of flaps A and B, and cut off the excess cardboard, as shown.

11 Remove tape from opposite end of box and repeat steps 3 to 10.

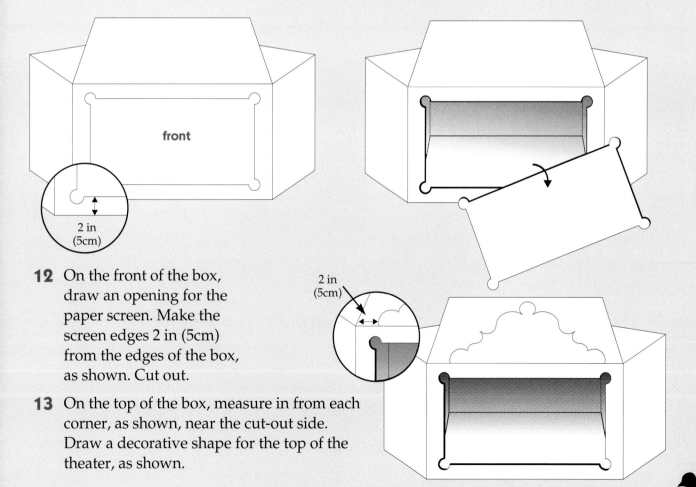

front

2 in
(5cm)

2 in
(5cm)

12 On the front of the box, draw an opening for the paper screen. Make the screen edges 2 in (5cm) from the edges of the box, as shown. Cut out.

13 On the top of the box, measure in from each corner, as shown, near the cut-out side. Draw a decorative shape for the top of the theater, as shown.

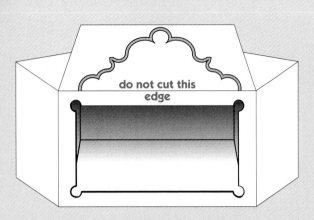

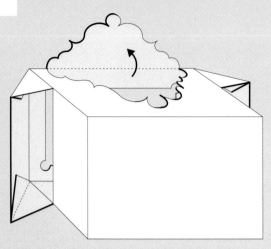

14 Cut around the top of the shape but do not cut across the front side of the box.

15 Turn the box around and fold the top shape forward.

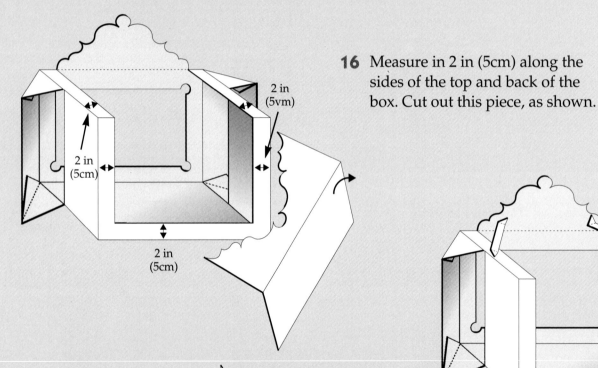

16 Measure in 2 in (5cm) along the sides of the top and back of the box. Cut out this piece, as shown.

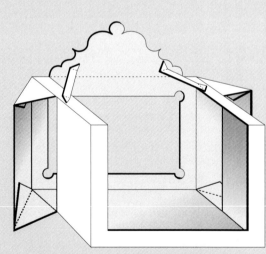

17 From discarded scraps of cardboard, cut two pieces of cardboard, as shown. Fold the two opposite corners, as shown.

18 Glue these strips to the back of the top shape and to the top edge of the box, as shown. This will hold the shape upright. Paint and shellac the front and wings of the theater. *See* photo, p86.

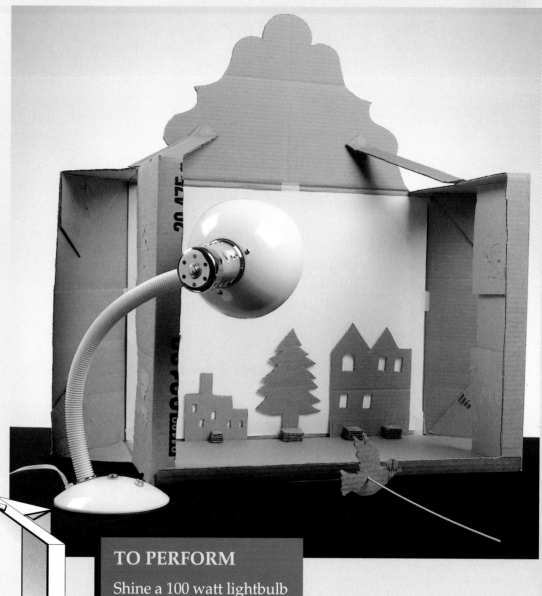

19 Cut a piece of white paper large enough to cover the front opening of the theater. Tape the paper to the inside front of the box, covering the opening.

TO PERFORM

Shine a 100 watt lightbulb or strong flashlight toward the back of the screen. The puppet player moves the puppet shapes across the back of paper screen. The shapes cast shadows on the screen and the audience watches the movements of the shadows.

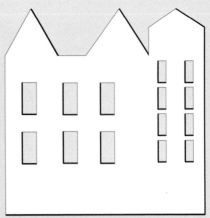

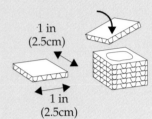

1 in
(2.5cm)

1 in
(2.5cm)

2 in
(5cm)

1 To make puppets, cut out shapes to suit your play from scraps of cardboard. Attach thin wooden sticks to the shapes with glue and tape.

2 Scenery is also cut from cardboard, and stands against the screen. Remember to add an extra 2 in (5cm) at the bottom of each piece to bring it up to the level of the paper screen.

3 To make the scenery stand up on its own, cut out 6 pieces of cardboard, as shown. Glue the pieces together one on top of another in a block. Make one block for each piece of scenery. Glue a block to the bottom of each scenery piece, as shown in the photograph.

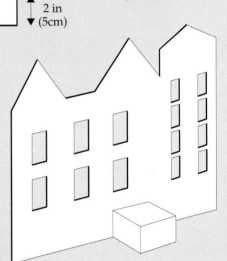

PUPPETS AND PROPS MATERIALS
cardboard
scissors
ruler
pencil
thin wooden sticks
glue
masking tape

Finishing Touches

TICKETS, POSTERS, TREAT BAGS, SERVING TRAY MATERIALS

bond paper (letter and legal size)
ruler
pencil
markers
photocopier
paint
brushes
sponge
scissors
brown paper lunch bags
cardboard box

TICKETS

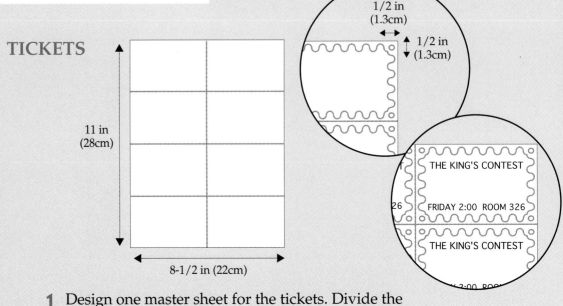

11 in (28cm)

8-1/2 in (22cm)

1/2 in (1.3cm)

1/2 in (1.3cm)

THE KING'S CONTEST
FRIDAY 2:00 ROOM 326
THE KING'S CONTEST

1 Design one master sheet for the tickets. Divide the paper into eight rectangles, as shown.

2 Draw a wavy border on each rectangle, as shown.

3 Write the name of the play, the time, and the date of the performance on each rectangle leaving a space in the center, as shown. This is the master sheet.

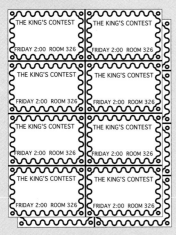

4 Photocopy the master sheet to make as many tickets as you need. Each copy will make eight tickets.

5 Cut a sponge into a shape to suit the play, for example, a king's crown or a frog's footprint.

6 Dip the sponge in paint and press the painted sponge in the space left on each rectangle.

7 When the paint is dry, cut each sheet into eight tickets.

POSTERS

14 in (36cm)

8-1/2 in (22cm)

1 To make a poster, draw a design on paper, as shown. Write the name of the play, the location, the date, and the time in the same way as for the tickets.

2 Photocopy as many posters as you need. Color or paint, as desired. Use the same ticket sponge print to decorate the border on the poster.

POPCORN AND PEANUT BAGS

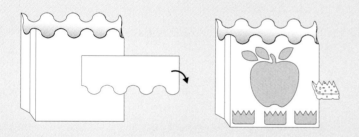

1 Cut a decorative edge on each lunch bag.

2 To decorate the bags, use the same sponge as used on the tickets and posters or cut sponges into popcorn or peanut shapes.

3 Dip the sponge in paint and press the sponge against the bag. Use thin paint because thick paint could fall off the bags when they dry. Do not shellac. *Always use non-toxic paint when decorating containers for food.*

SERVING TRAY

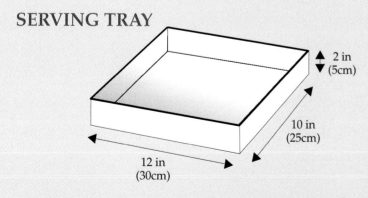

2 in (5cm)

10 in (25cm)

12 in (30cm)

1 Make a serving tray from a strong cardboard box, as shown. Cut the sides down, as shown. Paint.

2 Purchase colored paper cups for drinks, if desired.

Index